MW01078343

# About Island Press

Since 1984, the nonprofit organization Island Press has been stimulating, shaping, and communicating ideas that are essential for solving environmental problems worldwide. With more than 800 titles in print and some 40 new releases each year, we are the nation's leading publisher on environmental issues. We identify innovative thinkers and emerging trends in the environmental field. We work with world-renowned experts and authors to develop cross-disciplinary solutions to environmental challenges.

Island Press designs and executes educational campaigns in conjunction with our authors to communicate their critical messages in print, in person, and online using the latest technologies, innovative programs, and the media. Our goal is to reach targeted audiences—scientists, policymakers, environmental advocates, urban planners, the media, and concerned citizens—with information that can be used to create the framework for long-term ecological health and human well-being.

Island Press gratefully acknowledges major support of our work by The Agua Fund, The Andrew W. Mellon Foundation, Betsy & Jesse Fink Foundation, The Bobolink Foundation, The Curtis and Edith Munson Foundation, Forrest C. and Frances H. Lattner Foundation, G.O. Forward Fund of the Saint Paul Foundation, Gordon and Betty Moore Foundation, The Kresge Foundation, The Margaret A. Cargill Foundation, New Mexico Water Initiative, a project of Hanuman Foundation, The Overbrook Foundation, The S.D. Bechtel, Jr. Foundation, The Summit Charitable Foundation, Inc., V. Kann Rasmussen Foundation, The Wallace Alexander Gerbode Foundation, and other generous supporters.

The opinions expressed in this book are those of the author(s) and do not necessarily reflect the views of our supporters.

# Foundations of Real Estate Development Financing

*Metropolitan Planning + Design*
Series editors: Arthur C. Nelson and Reid Ewing

A collaboration between Island Press and the University of Utah's Department of City & Metropolitan Planning, this series provides a set of tools for students and professionals working to make our cities and metropolitan areas more sustainable, livable, prosperous, resilient, and equitable. As the world's population grows to nine billion by midcentury, the population of the United States will rise to half a billion. Along the way, the physical landscape will be transformed. Indeed, two-thirds of the built environment in the United States at midcentury will be constructed between now and then, presenting a monumental opportunity to reshape the places we live. The *Metropolitan Planning + Design* series presents an integrated approach to addressing this challenge, involving the fields of planning, architecture, landscape architecture, urban design, public policy, environmental studies, geography, and civil and environmental engineering. The series draws from the expertise of some of the world's leading scholars in the field of *Metropolitan Planning + Design*.

Please see Islandpress.org/Utah/ for more information.

Other books in the series:
*The TDR Handbook*, Arthur C. Nelson, Rick Pruetz, and Doug Woodruff (2011)
*Stewardship of the Built Environment*, Robert Young (2012)
*Planning as if People Matter*, Marc Brenman and Thomas W. Sanchez (2012)
*Good Urbanism: Six Steps to Creating Prosperous Places*, Nan Ellin (2012)
*Reshaping Metropolitan America*, Arthur C. Nelson (2013)
*Measuring Urban Design*, Reid Ewing and Otto Clemente (2013)

# Foundations of Real Estate Development Financing

## A Guide to Public-Private Partnerships

Arthur C. Nelson

Washington | Covelo | London

Copyright © 2014 Arthur C. Nelson

All rights reserved under International and Pan-American Copyright Conventions. No part of this book may be reproduced in any form or by any means without permission in writing from the publisher: Island Press, 2000 M Street, NW, Suite 650, Washington, DC 20036

ISLAND PRESS is a trademark of the Center for Resource Economics.

Library of Congress Cataloging-in-Publication Data

Nelson, Arthur C.
Foundations of real estate development financing : a guide to public-private partnerships / Arthur  C. Nelson.
pages cm.—(Metropolitan planning + design)
Includes bibliographical references and index.
ISBN 978-1-61091-561-8 (hardback)—ISBN 978-1-61091-562-5 (paper)—
ISBN 978-1-61091-563-2 (e-book)

1.  Real estate development—United States—Finance.
2.  Real estate development—United States.
3.  Public-private sector cooperation—United States.
4.  City planning—United States.  I. Title.

HD255.N45 2014
333.73'150681—dc23

2014004000

Printed on recycled, acid-free paper ♼

Manufactured in the United States of America

10 9 8 7 6 5 4 3 2 1

*Keywords*: Capitalization rate, commercial development, density, industrial development, infill, mixed-use development, net operating income (NOI), parking, nonresidential development, public-private partnerships, P3, real estate investment, redevelopment, residential development, return on investment (ROI), smart growth, successional development

To those academic leaders who supported my research and scholarship
in extraordinary ways during my academic career:

Brenda Case Scheer
Keith Bartholomew
John Randolph
Paul Knox
Steven P. French
David S. Sawicki
Fritz Wagner

To Dick Recht, who mentored me in real estate financial analysis and applied urban
economics early in my professional career as well as my academic career since

To Clark Ivory, who with his colleagues, mentored me on the private sector "P"
of public-private partnerships

And to the late Terry Holzheimer who was an inspiration to everyone in fashioning
successful public-private partnerships to reshape America

# Contents

# FOREWORD

Arthur C. Nelson has been our guide for the future development of the built environment in the United States for many years. The message is that the built environment is in the beginning stages of a fundamental structural shift, the first one since the mid-twentieth century. Sprawl is coming to an end, and the vast majority of new development will be the redevelopment of our center cities and the urbanization of existing suburbs, particularly the inner suburbs.

Future development will be higher density, mixed-use, and walkable. Yet, it will change the character of only a minority of our existing urbanized land, probably less than 10 percent of U.S. metropolitan land. Professor Nelson says in his introduction that most new development in the United States through 2030 "can easily occur on the parking lots of existing nonresidential development."

Local governments will be thrilled for this type of development to happen, since it will recycle declining drivable suburban development, abandoned factories, brownfields, and publicly owned land. The redevelopment will cut out declining, sometimes cancerous, decay while providing a much higher tax base, far more vital walkable urban places, and an increase in property values of surrounding property, especially if that property is single-family housing. Recent research has shown that high-density, walkable urban places increase the property values of nearby single-family housing by 40 to 100 percent on a price-per-square-foot basis compared to similar housing that is not within walking distance. This is why we are seeing NIMBYs becoming YIMBYs—"Yes, in my backyard" activists.

The reasons for local governments to encourage this redevelopment are now obvious. The question is how to do it, which is the focus of this book.

Experience with redevelopment of U.S. downtowns has shown that, when done successfully, for every $1 of public investment, there will be $10 to $15 of private investment. Hence, I tend to refer to the partnerships that are vital to this process and the focus of this book as "private-public" partnerships, reversing the order of this phrase. Professor Nelson uses the commonly used phrase, *public-private partnerships*, so as not to confuse, but the leadership role of the private sector cannot be forgotten.

The development or redevelopment process is a continuum of many steps, most of which occur prior to actual construction. The up-front community visioning, site acquisition, rezoning, planning, preliminary financial feasibility, and investment underwriting, among others, are the most risky in the entire process. As a result of this high risk, high returns are also generated. The local government is in the best position to maneuver these up-front development steps. Why? The local government is closest to the community, can provide needed convening and leadership, and has the most to gain. The returns for smart walkable urban development, when done successfully, can be so great that, in my experience, I have found no reason to subsidize redevelopment projects.

Public-private projects can be substantially helped by land assembly assistance provided by local government, by the contribution of city-owned land, by gaining community direction and support for higher-density mixed-use projects, and by obtaining patient equity, among other efforts. All of these resources can and should be invested in the projects. The returns should be at the same time as the developer partners' returns, which will be in the mid to long term. This will help the project move forward, to obtain financing easier and cheaper while keeping costs more affordable and also giving the local jurisdiction a return on its investment. This return could then be reinvested in future projects, like a revolving fund.

Professor Nelson's book gives the reader everything needed to engage in a complex public-private partnership, including the following:

- Market research and an understanding of trends
- The vocabulary necessary to understand and communicate
- The foundations of real estate investment analysis
- Tools in the public sector toolkit that contribute to public-private partnerships for redevelopment
- The power of patient equity

Professor Nelson expounds on and thoroughly explains the benefit of public-private partnerships in seizing the opportunities for commercial corridor and suburban center redevelopment—which is where he rightly sees the future of America's real estate investment. This text will be shown to be the invaluable go-to, how-to book for practitioners, students, and the private sector on redeveloping our built environment to meet the needs of future generations.

—Christopher B. Leinberger
Charles Bendit Distinguished Scholar
and Research Professor of Urban Real Estate
Chair, Center for Real Estate and Urban Analysis
George Washington University School of Business

# PREFACE

This book has been a lifetime in the making. Over the five decades in which I have been a professional and academic in planning and real estate development, I witnessed the two most severe recessions since the Great Depression along with the longest peacetime economic boom in the nation's history. I have also been engaged in various capacities with implementing federal planning and development policies undertaken during eight presidential administrations; indeed serving in two of them (presidents Bill Clinton and George W. Bush).

I cut my professional teeth as a planner and adviser to real estate investors during the late 1970s when mortgage rates hit 22 percent. In 1979, President Jimmy Carter appointed Paul Volcker as chair of the Federal Reserve Board. In this capacity, Volker squeezed inflation out of the economy but drove America into the deepest recession since the Great Depression. One of the first acts of President Ronald Reagan was to stimulate real estate investment through an impressive array of tax benefits relating to capital gains, accelerated depreciation, and other financial inducements. This was called the Economic Recovery Tax Act of 1981. About the same time, Congress, responding to President Reagan's request, relaxed regulation of the savings and loan industry, allowing them to wander away from home mortgages—in which they were experts—into commercial lending—in which they were neophytes. By the middle 1980s, America was awash with vacant, newly built structures because investors could actually make money after taxes by losing money in real estate.

In 1986, President Reagan and Congress saw the folly of artificially inducing real estate investment and changed the rules with the Tax Reform Act of 1986. It included such wholesale changes to real estate investment that the savings-and-loan industry collapsed; it also helped trigger the recession of

1990–91. By some estimates, the collapse of the savings and loan industry cost American taxpayers up to $300 billion and the nation's economy more than $1 trillion (in 2014 dollars). From the last part of George H. W. Bush's administration through that of President Bill Clinton's two terms, real estate investment soared, the federal budget became balanced, and the economy was generally robust yet stable.

President George W. Bush and Congress changed all that. Deep tax cuts wiped out federal surpluses, so debt soared. Home mortgage finance rules were relaxed and those that were not changed were not rigorously enforced. This allowed millions of homes to be financed through subprime mortgages (to people who would not otherwise qualify).

In 2006, I wrote of the vast oversupply of homes on large suburban lots relative to existing demand (Nelson 2006). By the late 2000s, the oversupply of homes depressed housing values, thereby putting millions of homes "under water" (where mortgage balances exceeded home values), which led in part to lending institutions' collapse—similar to the savings-and-loan collapse two decades earlier.[1] This helped trigger the Great Recession of 2007–2009 which was even more severe than the one two decades earlier. Combined with increasing joblessness and declining incomes, foreclosures soared. By the middle 2010s, housing values throughout most of the nation still had not reached levels seen a decade earlier. Effects of the Great Recession may linger well into the next decade if not longer.[2]

It is difficult to know what is in store for real estate investment over the next generation. But there is one thing I have observed as a constant through all of the real estate investment turmoil during my career: well-located property is more resilient to downturns and contributes more to sustained economic growth than fringe property. Unfortunately, underperforming property in attractive locations often prevents more efficient real estate investment for reasons I explain in chapter 1. New real estate investments are often diverted to second-best locations, making them vulnerable to economic downturns and by extension jeopardizing America's economic resilience.

The bottom line is that the public sector is needed when the private real estate market cannot seize efficient infill and redevelopment opportunities. The public sector has tools that can facilitate efficient private sector development. But the private sector is more efficient in producing, marketing, and managing real estate products than the public sector. The genius of public-private partnerships is that they generate more benefits mutually than either may do on their own.

The future of America's economic well-being cannot be relegated to the development of real estate products at second-best locations. We need public-private partnerships to facilitate the optimal redevelopment of commercial corridors, urban and suburban centers, and other aging, mostly nonresidential sites when redevelopment opportunities arise. Nothing less than the future of America's economy is at stake.

# Acknowledgments

I am indebted to hundreds of people over the past four decades who in many ways contributed to this book. Foremost are about three hundred students, mostly graduate students in planning, architecture, economic development, and urban design, who suffered through the programming of their own discounted cash models to test the viability of different public policy tools to leverage private investment in infill and redevelopment.

I am especially indebted to a number of individuals whom I note here in no particular order and with deepest apologies for being incomplete. Early in my career and since, I had the great fortune to be mentored in real estate finance and applied urban economics by J. Richard (Dick) Recht.

Christopher B. Leinberger, who wrote the foreword, and I have spent years comparing notes on how to structure public-private partnerships (P3s) to facilitate redevelopment. Although he rightfully calls them "private-public" partnerships for reasons given in his foreword, the order of nouns makes no difference when the outcome is as desired.

Several people with the firm RCLCO (Robert Charles Lesser Company) have helped shape my thinking on the role of P3s in facilitating redevelopment, and I suppose I have helped shape theirs. With apologies for being incomplete, they include Gregg Logan, Gadi Kauffman, Melina Duggal, Shyam Kannan (now with the Washington Metropolitan Area Transportation Authority), and Taylor Mammen.

Alex Joyce, Leila Aman, C. J. Gabbe, Alex Steinberger, and John Fregonese at Fregonese Associates have been especially helpful in making this book happen. I am in their debt for the cover art as well as for two case studies with images that illuminate how the public partner can leverage private redevelopment. Together with Dejan Eskic, we created a rate-of-return application for the Envision Tomorrow Plus (ET+) scenario planning, open-source software package, that can be accessed at http://www.arch.utah.edu/cgi-bin/wordpress-etplus/. The theme of this book started with my first academic appointment at Kansas State University (1984–1986), where I learned how Manhattan, Kansas, then under the leadership of Gary Stith, created a series of public-private partnerships (P3s) to redevelop the east end of its main street into a retail mall anchoring redevelopment investment along the main street and northward. Today, thirty years later, the vision has become reality. Small town America can learn much from Manhattan's experience.

At the University of New Orleans (1986–1987), Fritz Wagner, then dean of the School of Urban and Public Affairs, introduced me to many in the development community engaged in infill and redevelopment throughout the metropolitan area. Given its land constraints, few metropolitan areas depend more on infill and redevelopment than metropolitan New Orleans.

Many of my ideas were honed while on the faculty of city and regional planning at the Georgia Institute of Technology (1987–2002). Upon my arrival, I took over a course called Urban Development Methods from Richard Dagenhart, who had developed basic real estate finance tools in Lotus (the predecessor to currently popular spreadsheet packages such as Microsoft Excel). I also learned much from Larry Keating, who, with me, comanaged Georgia Tech's joint master of city and regional planning degree with Georgia State University's graduate real estate certificate. One of my students at Georgia Tech, Laura S. Davis, refined many of those early Lotus models that were later converted into Excel.

I also learned much about how the "public" part of P3s works from Paul Kelman, then vice president of Central Atlanta Progress, and later from Jennifer Ball, a former student who serves now in a similar capacity and who supplied the Atlanta case study.

In 2000, I served as a special adviser to Susan M. Wachter, the assistant secretary for policy development and research for the U.S. Department of Housing and Urban Development in the Clinton Administration. Many at HUD helped further shape my perspectives on the public role in P3s, including James E. Hoben, Edwin A. Stromberg, David Engel, and Victor Rubin (now at PolicyLink). I continued my service in the Bush administration through much of 2001.

Shortly after my HUD service, I relocated from Georgia Tech to found Virginia Tech's urban affairs and planning program at its Alexandria Center (2002–2008). It was there that I learned much about crafting effective P3s from the late Terry Holzheimer, then director of Arlington Economic Development. He provided me with the Shirlington case study found in the introduction a scant few weeks before his passing. I also founded the Planning Academy at Virginia Tech, where I taught courses in P3s. Robert Lang, the founding director of the Metropolitan Institute at Virginia Tech, where I later served as codirector, acquainted me with the sheer vastness of commercial corridor, suburban center, and dispersed nonresidential development which has since become a central theme in my academic and professional work.

Through the 2000s, I received considerable support and encouragement for my work from Bruce Katz, Robert Puentes, and Amy Liu at the Brookings Institution to "connect the dots" converting aging nonresidential spaces into vibrant new places.

Ellen Dunham-Jones at Georgia Tech and June Williamson at The City College of New York have given me additional insights through their focus on rebuilding bland suburban centers into robust, mixed-use places.

I give a special thanks to Joe Molinaro at the National Association of Realtors for his sustained encouragement of my line of thinking going on two decades, and for his especially keen edits and insights from an earlier version of this book. The NAR community preference surveys of 2004, 2011, and 2013 reinforce my views of how future markets will be very different from those of the past.

With the offer of a presidential professorship, I joined the faculty at the University of Utah (2008–2014) where I founded its Metropolitan Research Center (MRC), a doctoral degree in metropolitan planning, policy, and design, and its master of real estate development degree. Deans Brenda Scheer of the College of Architecture + Planning and Taylor Randall of the David Eccles School of Business were instrumental in championing and then helping manage those new initiatives.

I was attracted to Utah in large part by the pioneering visioning processes led by Robert Grow to shape the future of the Wasatch Front. I knew that redevelopment would play a crucial role in Utah's future, so what better place to study redevelopment than where it is needed? Soon after arriving, I became good friends with the president and other key officials of Ivory Homes and ICO Inc., Utah's (and one of the nation's) largest infill and redevelopment firms. Even though communities will benefit immensely from infill and redevelopment, challenges exist in making it happen. Clark Ivory (president), Jim Seaberg, Chris Gamvroulas, and David Zollinger gave me unique insights into those challenges.

In 2010, a consortium of interests was formed to compete for a grant offered by HUD's Sustainable Communities program. That consortium comprised Salt Lake County (headed by David White and Michael Gallegos), Envision Utah (initially headed by Alan Matheson, who went on to serve in the governor's office, and later by Robert Grow and Ari Bruening), the Wasatch Front Regional Council (headed by Andrew Gruber and later joined by Ted Knowlton), the Mountainlands Association of Governments (led by Shaun Seager), the Utah Chapter of the American Planning Association (led by John Janson), and the MRC.

We were fortunate to win a grant to help implement Wasatch Choice for 2040. A key part of implementation was creating tools comparing outcomes between alternative scenarios for local areas. Two tools—one for estimating redevelopment opportunity timing and the other for estimating the rate of return from different redevelopment scenarios—are based substantially on work that led to this book. We are all indebted to key HUD officials for giving us this opportunity, especially Shelley Poticha (now at the Natural Resources Defense Council) and Mariia Zimmermann (now in private practice).

I owe further thanks to Matt Miller, one of my doctoral students at Utah, who created some of the figures and land-use analyses used in this book and, more importantly, helped me pioneer the redevelopment opportunity timing model; to Kathy Kittrell, another doctoral student, for synthesizing development types; and to Allison Spain, the MRC program manager, for providing additional figures and editing earlier versions of this book.

I specially thank Dejan Eskic, a research analyst for the MRC, who worked closely with me to refine the redevelopment model and then codevelop the Excel workbook that accompanies this book, of which he is coauthor.

Another thanks to Toby Rattner and Katie Kramer, president and vice president, respectively, of the Council of Development Finance Agencies, for their very special assistance in helping this book meet the needs of public–private partnerships engaged in infill and redevelopment.

I owe a very large debt to Heather Boyer of Island Press for managing the process and contributing key editorial direction, and to Sharis Simonian for managing the copy editing process

A final thanks to Monika Nelson for carefully proofreading the final draft.

And to everyone else who helped me shape my ideas over the years: Thank you.

## Introduction

# The Future of America Is Redevelopment, and the Future of Redevelopment Is Public-Private Partnerships

America is a suburban nation: it is where most Americans live. American suburbs are mostly low-density landscapes with segregated land uses that are overwhelmingly dependent on the automobile. A growing number of preference surveys indicate that half or more of Americans want something different. Most would trade large lots for smaller ones or for attached homes if their neighborhoods were walkable, had a variety of housing options, were within a short drive of key destinations, and had meaningful transit options (Logan et al. 2007; Nelson 2013b). Aging boomers especially want those features in their suburbs (Nelson 2010). Meeting emerging market preferences in suburbs may be difficult because most suburbs are substantially built out.

Nonetheless, important opportunities exist to redevelop America's extensive networks of commercial corridors and suburban centers. I estimate that America has about twelve thousand square miles of land, an area equivalent to the states of Connecticut and New Jersey, that are used for surface parking, loading, storage, and other nonstructural uses. The supply of this land is so vast that nearly all of America's new nonresidential spaces and nearly all new multilevel attached residential units can easily occur on the parking lots of existing nonresidential development (Nelson 2013a), especially along commercial corridors and in suburban centers.

An unprecedented opportunity exists to meet the needs of this emerging market and to realize many other benefits by simply reshaping that which is already built, because much of this land has attributes that make it ideal for redevelopment:

- These sites are already flat and are reasonably well drained, so this part of the development process is largely finished.
- Almost all of these sites sit along major highways with four or more lanes, often with wide rights-of-way for easements. Because they are along multilane corridors that connect urban and suburban nodes, these sites are "transit-ready."
- Large-scale utilities run along those major highways and are easily accessed for upgrading, if needed. As they age, these utilities will need to be replaced. The conundrum facing local government is whether to approve new greenfield development where initial utility capital costs are low or to brace for the upgrades of major utility infrastructure along built-out corridors that would have to be done anyway and at lower long-term cost per unit of service delivery. Prudent fiscal management would seem to favor the latter investment decision.
- Prior development approvals have already committed these sites to uses other than low-density residential development.
- These sites have motivated owners who are interested in maximizing their return. This is important because impediments to redevelopment include the inability to assemble multiple small ownerships, gaining the confidence of owners and showing that it is in their best interest to redevelop, and acquiring clear title. This is not the case with most large, commercially developed sites.
- As these sites age, the deterioration of structures compromises the value of nearby residential property.
- Those residential property owners may be motivated to simultaneously deflect development pressure away from their neighborhoods into aging commercial sites, especially if they have a constructive say in how they are redeveloped. In other words, potential NIMBYs (not-in-my-backyard) may become YIMBYs (yes-in-my-backyard).

Moreover, the redevelopment of aging warehouses, industrial buildings, commercial corridors, and suburban centers generates the following benefits (Port of Portland et al. 2004):

- Reclaims underused space and establishes new growth in areas with existing infrastructure
- Improves water quality and makes riverfronts more accessible to pedestrians and for recreational purposes
- Preserves historic, cultural, or social icons important to community identity
- Supports a variety of businesses, interests, and needs of the community
- Facilitates mixed-use developments, which provide high-density housing that helps to prevent sprawl and conserve natural resources, agricultural land, and forests by concentrating development
- Improves environmental health through remediation of degraded and contaminated buildings and land
- Reduces auto dependency by concentrating development to cultivate healthier communities while mitigating greenhouse gas emissions
- Converts areas that are a drain on taxes and municipal services into financial assets through improved property values, higher property taxes, and, often, new sources of revenue
- Produces employment opportunities for local workers (which can change commuting behavior)
- Encourages surrounding property owners to reinvest, making their properties more valuable and typically resulting in a higher tax yield for the community

If the opportunity is so great and the benefits so plentiful, why do we see so few examples of suburban redevelopment occurring? For one thing, examples are scattered across the nation, mostly on a parcel-by-parcel basis. The examples reported in Sobel and Bodzin (2002), Dunham-Jones and Williamson (2011), and Williamson (2013) are mostly not very large scale and are spread across suburban landscapes. Furthermore, few developers have the appetite or resources to redevelop large parcels of fifty or one hundred or two hundred acres. Although the redevelopment of the occasional regional mall garners headlines, the vast majority of redevelopment is practically imperceptible on an annual basis but is transformative over decades.

The stakes are high. Between 2010 and 2040, $30 trillion (or more than half of all construction spending in the United States) will be for redeveloping the existing built environment. At least half of this expenditure will be for the redevelopment of commercial corridors and in suburban centers. But if new development is steered to greenfields where new infrastructure has to be installed, local governments will have two sets of infrastructure systems to finance: the existing system, which will need to be upgraded probably sooner rather than later, and the new system serving low-density, segregated land uses. More to the point: studies by such groups as the Urban Land Institute (ULI) and the National Association of Industrial and Office Parks (NAIOP) show that redevelopment generates higher returns to investors. It seems clear that the future of America's built landscape will be the redevelopment of its privately owned real estate.

America's future, therefore, depends on public-private partnerships to facilitate redevelopment. Even though redevelopment generates higher rates of investment return to investors, numerous obstacles have to be overcome. Some of these involve changing planning and development codes to be more responsive to redevelopment opportunities. Others are expensive in the near term because infrastructure has to be upgraded— though it would probably have to be upgraded eventually anyway. Many involve land assembly brownfield remediation. Still others are related to the complexity of modern real estate financing, especially when it involves multiple land uses.

Public-private partnerships, or P3s, are contractual relationships between public and private entities to facilitate real estate development. They can include the repurposing of existing real estate development through rehabilitation to change an original function, such as converting warehouses into residential lofts. It can also include the removal of existing structures, land assembly, infrastructure upgrades, and related activities to redevelop areas and sites. There are many forms of P3s, most of which engage the private sector in building, operating, maintaining, or owning and leasing back facilities to the public or nonprofit sectors.[1] The kind of P3 used in this book is one in which the public sector facilitates private real estate development in targeted "redevelopment" areas.

Each party contributes to the partnership what it does best. For the public sector, this can include the following:

- Planning and zoning activities that can recast the overall development vision of an area
- Upgrading infrastructure
- Expanding mobility options through sidewalks, bikeways, road improvements, and transit
- Acquiring property and preparing it for redevelopment
- Assisting with financing

For the private sector, it can include these elements:

- Market analysis
- Construction financing
- Construction management
- Procurement of long-term financing
- Project leasing and property management

Public-private partnerships facilitate development that would not occur without one partner or the other.

There must be a public purpose justifying P3s, however, because spending public resources for strictly private gain is inappropriate. Public purposes can include low- or moderate-income housing, new jobs, redevelopment of underinvested areas, and economic development. Such partnerships advance local economic development, stabilize communities, improve the local tax base, and reward private investors.

Above all, keep in mind that the purpose of real estate development is to make money.[2] Without profit, there are no resources to enter into new development ventures, let alone pay the bills to stay in business, whether in the public, private, or nonprofit sectors.

We have entered into a period of U.S. history in which there may be more redevelopment of the built environment than development of greenfields. This book, *Foundations of Real Estate Development Financing: A Guide to Public-Private Partnerships*, shows how real estate finance tools combined with planning and implementation by public-private partnerships can facilitate the redevelopment of the United States. A key feature of this book is an Excel workbook that is available online at no cost at http://islandpress.org/ReshapeMetroAmerica. Appendix A of this book provides an overview of the Excel workbook for users.

The book and workbook are intended for use by planners, economic development professionals, public officials, engaged citizens, and students. The book is also a primer for real estate professionals and students on the tools that may be available to leverage private real estate investment, how they work, and under what circumstances they are appropriate. Through case studies, the book shows how the public and private sectors are both winners through public-private partnerships.

One example of a successful public-private partnership is the Village at Shirlington, an aging retail and service area in Arlington County, Virginia. It shows how both the public and the private sectors worked as partners to transform the village into something special.

## The Village at Shirlington, Arlington County, Virginia

Shirlington comprises about sixty acres west of I-395 and south of Four Mile Run creek, just minutes from downtown Washington, DC. It was the location of metropolitan Washington's first shopping center in the late 1940s and was a conventional suburban shopping center that included a grocery store, auto shops, a big box, and several other small shops. The combination of multiple lots, inadequate infrastructure, and a lack of vision prevented it from being redeveloped by the private sector alone (see fig. 0.1a).

Terry Holzheimer (2008) reviews the public-private redevelopment process. Arlington County undertook a series of planning processes engaging community interests and then prepared and adopted the Shirlington Phased Development Site Plan (PDSP) with the Shirlington Design Guidelines in the late 1990s. The PDSP established the land uses along with their densities and intensities, as well as building heights, transportation facilities,

**Figure 0.1a.** Shirlington, Virginia, before redevelopment. (Credit: Arlington Economic Development)

**Figure 0.1b.** Shirlington, Virginia, after redevelopment. (Credit: Arlington Economic Development)

utility improvements, and expanded community facilities. The design guidelines called for a main street with pedestrian-friendly access plus a comprehensive planning element. The overall plan called for a major theater; expansion of the Shirlington Library, including a public plaza; and numerous street amenities, such as plantings, outdoor restaurants, signage and lighting, street furniture, and storefronts with high degrees of window transparency, which engages pedestrians and invites them into the stores and restaurants. Plans also called for nearly 2,500 parking spaces distributed behind commercial buildings with entrances from several streets which improved pedestrian flow and safety. (see fig. 0.1b)

A key element of the overall plan was a partnership between the county and Street Retail, Inc., for the redevelopment of Shirlington. The partnership included these elements:

- Fiscal impact analysis and assessment of the county's investment alternatives relating to the site
- Land exchange and land lease
- Environmental remediation
- County financial commitments
- Agreements on operations and maintenance
- Agreements on amounts, collection, and use of parking fees
- Construction of a county library and live-theater facility
- A grocery store
- County participation in a share of the project's income

Through a series of other development agreements with Federal Realty Investment Trust, the largest landowner in the area, the Village at Shirlington was substantially built out during the 2000s. By the early 2010s, it had nearly 600,000 square feet of office and nearly 300,000 square feet of retail space, more than 1,000 residential units, and 142 hotel rooms. It also includes 134 on-street parking spaces and more than 2,400 off-street parking spaces in surface lots and garages. Four of the village's garages provide daytime parking for offices, with evening, weekend, and holiday parking for public use. The county estimates that, for every dollar it put into the project, another $42 was invested by the private sector. In 2010, total tax revenues exceeded $8 million.

# Chapter 1

# The Cycle of Development, Optimal Redevelopment, Redevelopment Goals and Benefits, and Barriers to Redevelopment

Before I review the foundations of real estate development finance and the role of public-private partnerships in redeveloping the United States, I need to show where P3s fit in the development/redevelopment cycle. I start by describing the cycle of urban development and what I call "efficient redevelopment." This is followed by a review of impediments to efficient development, and I conclude with the role of P3s to facilitate efficient redevelopment.

## The Cycle of Development

That urban areas transform themselves over time is certain. Miles Colean (1953) calls this the "cycle of development." Larry S. Bourne (1967) provides a succinct review of the process, which comprises an initial period of construction followed by a period of increasing value and function, then a period of increasing maintenance costs and deterioration, perhaps leading to idling or abandonment, and then a period of redevelopment as the old structures are replaced.

Consider the normal life of a building. It is built initially to serve an investment horizon and becomes obsolete either because of economic factors (where the building is more expensive to maintain than justified by revenue streams) or functionality (where markets have changed, leaving the building unsuitable for its initial use) or both. As the structure loses value through a process called

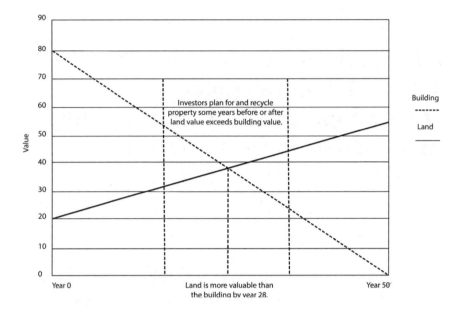

**Figure 1.1.** Optimal timing of redevelopment for a fifty-year structure assuming land value appreciates 2 percent annually, compounded, net of inflation. (In the public domain; created by Arthur C. Nelson and redrawn by Allison Spain)

depreciation, the land on which it sits will normally gain value, especially if the urban area is growing.

Figure 1.1 illustrates this appreciation in land and depreciation in the structure assuming a new building is built with a fifty-year useful life, which is common for one- and two-floor office buildings. When its doors open, the building accounts for 80 percent of the property value and the land for the remaining 20 percent; this is a typical building-to-land relationship for commercial buildings. The building depreciates over a fifty-year period, or 1.6 percent annually, and becomes worthless (except for any scrap value) in the fiftieth year. Land, on the other hand, gains value at about the rate of growth of the urban area, compounded. If the population or employment growth rate is 2 percent annually, the land value increases at this rate (net of inflation). By the twenty-eighth year, the land is worth more than the building. Some years before and after this happens, the investors reassess their investment and, ideally, renew the site by replacing the initial structure with one consistent with the highest and best use over a new investment horizon.

For the most part, nonresidential space is not durable. Overall, the United States has about 100 billion square feet of enclosed space used for such nonresidential purposes as retail, offices, institutions, and so forth. About 70 percent of all nonresidential space is housed in buildings of one or two floors. In any given year, about 2.5 billion square feet of nonresidential space becomes idled or is replaced—2.5 percent annually.

In contrast, residential structures are quite durable. The United States has about 130 million residential units, but only 500,000 residential units— about 0.5 percent—become vacant or are replaced each year. I have estimated that the typical residential unit lasts about 170 years (Nelson 2004, 2013a). Pitkin and Myers (2008) estimate that units last 200 to 500 years. Whatever the length, planners and public officials need to understand that residential development is very durable, not because the structures themselves are built to last a long time, but because occupants will maintain the unit through repairs and rehabilitation for decades or even centuries. Most nonresidential development, in contrast, is not durable and needs to be replaced about every 20 to 40 years.

Urbanized land thus goes through a series of changes over decades and centuries. The first building on a site, for instance, might be a neighborhood grocery store. As the building ages, it becomes more expensive to maintain, so profit (revenue net of costs) goes down. In the meantime, the land value goes up. The "opportunity" cost of keeping the land in its current use goes up as profit in the current use goes down. At some point, the landowner incurs the cost of demolition and rebuilding to increase profits by going to the "highest and best" use of the land. Maybe the new structure is a low-rise retail store. In a few more decades, the next highest and best use might be a midrise office building. In theory, redevelopment of the built environment would be seamless, leading to ever higher and better uses over time, as illustrated in figure 1.2. In practice, this is rarely the case, for reasons I outline next.

## Optimal Redevelopment

The first buildings to be constructed in an area are often small and built of material that is easy to dismantle. At some point, buildings become of such

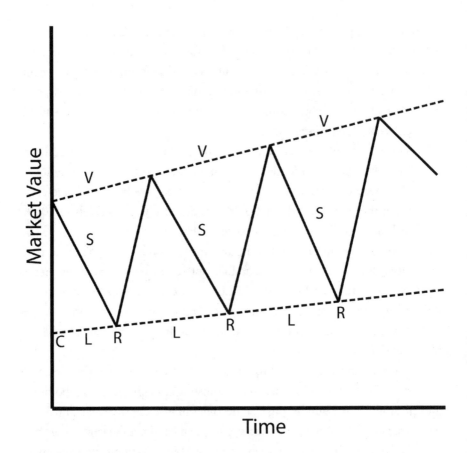

L is the value of land
V is the highest and best use value of the developed property
C is the initial construction cost
R is the redevelopment cost including demolition
S is the structure value reflecting depreciation

**Figure 1.2.** The cycle of urban redevelopment. (In the public domain; created by Arthur C. Nelson and redrawn by Allison Spain)

size and durability that they may be difficult to replace, especially if market conditions do not warrant the expense of both dismantling and rebuilding the site. The result can be what Bourne (1967) calls a "constrained" process of redevelopment. This could lead to blight as the structure becomes idled or vacant and its presence discourages reinvestment in the area, thereby delaying redevelopment beyond that which is "optimal."

In a classic paper theorizing the optimal timing of redevelopment, Donald Shoup (1970, 43) demonstrated that the optimal time for redevelopment of urban land depends on four factors:

> The optimal date for development or redevelopment of urban land depends on (1) the discount rate applying in the real estate market, (2) the property tax rate, (3) the earnings in any interim use, and (4) the way in which the highest and best use of the land is expected to change in the future.

I refine Shoup's principles for application in this book. The first is the "discount rate" that is applicable to the local real estate market. Put simply, this is the rate at which future revenues net of costs ("profit") are discounted to the present to allow for a fair comparison of alternative investment choices. A high discount rate means the investor is willing to pay less for something, presumably because risks are higher.

The discount rate is akin to the capitalization rate, or "cap rate," which is the ratio between the net operating income (NOI) of a real estate investment (rental income less operating expenses) and its market value: NOI/value. If the NOI is $100,000 and the building has a value of $1 million, the cap rate is 0.10 ($100,000/$1 million). If the building has a value of $2 million, the cap rate is 0.05. Generally, the higher the capitalization rate is, the sooner redevelopment will occur. This is because the higher the cap rate, the lower the value of real estate, and thus the more attractive it is for redevelopment. (I discuss capitalization rate mechanics in the "Real Estate Finance Concepts" section in chapter 3.)

Generally, the market determines the cap rate, so the key variable in estimating value is the NOI. If the NOI goes down, perhaps because taxes go up or rents go down (as the building deteriorates with age), the building value goes down. As value declines but the local market is stable or growing, the optimal time of redevelopment will occur sooner rather than later.

Related to the NOI is the second redevelopment factor: the level of property taxes. Property taxes are considered an expense, so the higher the taxes, the lower the NOI, and therefore the lower the value and the more likely a site may be redeveloped. Hence, one outcome of high property taxes is accelerated redevelopment, whereas a lower rate may defer it.

The optimal use of land will be affected by Shoup's third factor: the earnings in any interim use preceding the next highest and best use. If there is little or no income, the optimal timing of development will be accelerated, but if there is enough revenue from an interim use, optimal redevelopment will be delayed. Using the case of downtown surface parking lots, I will demonstrate how inefficient property taxes can increase earnings from interim uses of land, thereby raising the NOI and deferring the optimal timing of redevelopment.

Property taxes are an important part of real estate investment decisions. Nationally, property taxes average about 1 percent of the market value of property, though there is wide variation among states and local governments. One percent on a $1 million commercial property would be $10,000 annually. If the NOI is $100,000, the property tax would be equivalent to 10 percent of net revenue.

Property taxes are based on the value of property, but "value" can mean many things. The value of a home that sells for $100,000 would be considered $100,000, and it would be taxed accordingly. If a home does not sell for decades, its value would be estimated, and ideally that value would be equivalent to what it would sell for and it would be taxed accordingly. Although this seems straightforward, its application to income-producing property gets complex.

Suppose there is an acre of vacant land in the middle of downtown. Its property taxes would be based on its estimated sales price. If nearby lots sold for $1 per square foot, this acre would be worth perhaps $4,356,000 and it would be taxed accordingly. A 1 percent tax rate means the owner would need to pay $43,560 annually in property taxes.

The owner may wisely convert this vacant piece of land into a surface parking lot. Capital costs are mostly putting asphalt over the land and building an attendant's shack. Operating costs are just the attendants and their benefits, a business license, modest grounds keeping, and property taxes. But instead of paying $43,560 in taxes, the local property tax assessor values the parking lot based on its current use ("use-value") and not the market value of the property. To calculate the use-value of the parking lot, the assessor applies the capitalization rate to the parking lot NOI. The example of this appears in the top half of table 1.1. The use-value would be $278,421, or about 6 percent of the market value of land. At 1 percent, the property taxes would be $2,784, not $43,560. Thanks to property tax policy, the interim use generates sufficient cash flow to carry the property.

**Table 1.1.**
The Economics of a Downtown Surface Parking Lot Based on Use-Value and Market-Value Property Taxation

| Measure | Use-Value Taxation: When Parking Lots Are Subsidized through the Property Tax Structure | Land and Improvement Taxation: When Parking Lots Are Not Subsidized through the Property Tax Structure |
| --- | --- | --- |
| Acre of land in square feet | 43,560 | 43,560 |
| Average parking lot area at 19 feet by 9 feet plus access | 342 | 342 |
| Parking spaces per acre | 127 | 127 |
| Per-month parking revenue per space | $100 | $100 |
| Total annual revenue per acre | $152,842 | $152,842 |
| Expenses | $125,000 | $125,000 |
| Net operating income | $27,842 | $27,842 |
| Capitalization rate for parking lots (see chap. 3) | 0.1 | — |
| Capitalized value | $278,421 | — |
| Value of central business district land in its highest and best use at $100/square foot | — | $4,356,000 |
| Property tax rate | 1.00% | 1.00% |
| Property tax assessment | $2,784 | $43,560 |
| Net income after property taxes with subsidies | $25,058 | ($15,718) |

But what if the policy defers redevelopment beyond that which is optimal? The property owners have little incentive to sell and all the incentive to wait until the market value of their property rises to such a high level that they become willing to sell. In the meantime, the development that would have occurred but for the property tax policy does not occur or, worse, is deflected elsewhere into places where such development is suboptimal. Development patterns would thus be skewed. The property owners themselves could be considered speculators, as their holding costs are artificially low, essentially being subsidized by other payers of property tax. When they sell, they would receive speculative as opposed to normal gains (Shoup 1970, 44).

In contrast, suppose this parking lot were assessed taxes based on its market value as opposed to its use-value. This situation is shown in table 1.1. The owners would incur a loss of $15,718. Unless they are willing to pay those losses year after year, they may be induced into developing or selling to a developer. Development would thus be optimal. A few cities have moved from use-value to market-value property tax systems in their downtowns, with desired effects (see Oates and Schwab 1996).

The last factor relates to expectations of what the highest and best use of property may be in the future. An owner of property may choose to keep it undeveloped (or underdeveloped as an interim use) until the market favors a much more intensely developed project—perhaps a high-rise tower surrounded by lower-rise offices and residential buildings. During the U.S. suburbanization process, for instance, some landowners decided to wait until low-density residential development surrounded their parcel and would then build a shopping center serving those new households. The owners may risk waiting too long to develop, however, as markets change over time.

## Planning Goals for and the Benefits of Redevelopment

In my view, redevelopment should be based on meeting these five planning goals (see Nelson and Duncan 1995), which are described further in the following sections:

- Maximizing environmental quality[1]
- Minimizing the cost of publicly provided facilities and services
- Maximizing land-use interactions
- Fairly distributing the benefits of development
- Elevating the quality of life

## Maximizing Environmental Quality

Maximizing environmental quality does not necessarily mean development must have no adverse environmental outcomes. What it does mean is maximizing it within the context of meeting other societal needs, such as real estate development. Two key environmental benefits associated with redeveloping existing places rather than developing greenfields are (1) preserving open space so as to continue receiving ecosystem service benefits and (2) reducing carbon emissions so as to improve air quality and reduce the pace of climate change.

In my book *Reshaping Metropolitan America* (Nelson 2013b), I estimated that there are enough parking lots to support all new and redeveloped nonresidential needs and all multifamily development needs for the United States; in some fast-growing metropolitan areas, however, this is not the case. I also estimated that if all new residential and nonresidential development occurred on greenfields, roughly 15 million acres of land would be consumed. Using analysis reported by Mertens and Rubinchik (2006), I estimated that the present value cost in lost ecosystem service benefits would be about $4 trillion over the next century. If all development occurred on parking lots, this figure would be much lower, arguably even zero.

Moreover, if all new development occurs on existing developed land, two things happen to the consumption of fossil fuels. First, miles traveled per vehicle may go down because the outward spread of urbanization is halted. Second, new development on existing developed parcels can reduce the distances between origin and destination. As the number of vehicle miles traveled (VMT) is reduced, so are the greenhouse gases that science has found to influence global climate change (see Ewing et al. 2008). I estimated that, when infill and redevelopment projects are coordinated, the cumulative and synergistic air emissions reductions range up to 40 percent without transit options and up to 50 percent with them.

## Minimizing the Cost of Publicly Provided Facilities and Services

An extensive literature shows that the costs of delivering a large range of public facilities and services vary by the location, density, and configuration or mix of development (see Nelson, Bowles, et al. 2008; Nelson 2013b). The same number of users, for instance, can be served by a ten-inch water main extending one mile or ten miles, but the cost to serve those users over ten miles is literally ten times more expensive than serving the users over one mile. This would not be an issue if users paid fees or taxes based on the actual cost to extend facilities to their properties. I call this "full cost" charges. Unfortunately, most locally provided facilities are financed based on "average" cost charges. The result is that high-cost development is subsidized by low-cost development with the perverse effect that over time there is more high-cost and less low-cost development (see also Blais 2010). Local community costs increase, as must local taxes and other revenues to pay for them. The long-term outcome is inefficient development patterns.

Table 1.2 illustrates this for Albuquerque, New Mexico. During the middle 2000s, studies in Albuquerque showed that little or no new investment was needed to accommodate growth in some parts of the city, while other parts required new facilities to accommodate new development (see Nelson, Bowles, et al. 2008). City-operated facilities include public safety, parks, recreation and trails, drainage, and streets.[2] Table 1.2 shows the difference in "net" costs needed to serve the same kind of development in what the city calls its fully served area but which is better characterized as the infill/redevelopment area of the city compared to what the city calls its "partially served" area, which is better characterized as the greenfield area of the city. Net costs are the new costs to service new development less the new tax and fee revenue it generates. Clearly, it would cost the city much less to accommodate development in the infill/redevelopment area than in the greenfield area. Unfortunately, its facility financing system does just the opposite by subsidizing higher-cost development by overcharging lower-cost development. Albuquerque thus gets more high-cost and less low-cost development as a result.

## Maximizing Land-Use Interactions

I also showed in Reshaping Metropolitan America (Nelson 2013b) that more densely developed areas with more mixed uses and more transportation options were more productive than less densely developed areas with segregated land uses and few alternatives to the automobile. A key purpose of redevelopment is to increase development density and to broaden the land-use mix, ideally taking advantage of existing, new, or planned transit systems.

**Table 1.2.**

Net Capital Costs to Accommodate New Development in Two Areas and Citywide for Albuquerque, New Mexico

| Land Use | Unit | Infill/ Redevelopment Area | Greenfield Area | Citywide Average |
|---|---|---|---|---|
| Single-family | Dwelling | $1,366 | $7,775 | $5,978 |
| Multifamily | Dwelling | $591 | $3,315 | $3,017 |
| Retail under 100,000 square feet | 1,000 sf | $455 | $4,542 | $3,167 |
| Office 50,000–100,000 square feet | 1,000 sf | $100 | $4,524 | $3,167 |
| Business park | 1,000 sf | $100 | $3,881 | $3,167 |

*Source:* Adapted from Nelson, Bowles, et al. (2008) and Duncan and Associates (2012). Figures for single-family units assume a 2,000-square-foot home on a 10,000-square-foot lot, with 2,500 square feet of impervious surface area.

Reid Ewing and colleagues (Ewing and Hamidi 2014) have created a Compactness Index that measures land-use interactions, which I use to compare outcomes among key measures of economic vitality. The Ewing Compactness Index[3] comprises fourteen measures organized into four factors (density, mixed use, centering, and street accessibility):

*Density* (six measures)

    Gross density of urban and suburban census tracts

    Percentage of the population living at low suburban densities (fewer than 1,500 persons per square mile)

    Percentage of the population living at medium to high urban densities (greater than 12,500 persons per square mile)

    Urban density based on the National Land Cover Database

    Density of the densest population center to which county block groups relate

    Gross employment density of urban and suburban census tracts

*Mixed Use* (three measures)

    Job–population balance (tract)

    Service job–population balance (tract)

Degree of job mixing as the countywide average degree of job mixing

*Centering* (three measures)
Coefficient of variation in census block group population densities
Coefficient of variation in census block group employment densities
Percentage of the county population relating to at least one population center

*Street Accessibility* (two measures)
Intersection density for urban and suburban census tracts within the county
Percentage of four-or-more-way intersections for urban and suburban census tracts

Like an IQ score, the higher the Ewing Compactness Index score is, the more integrated and synergistic the area measured is compared to the mean (based on an index of 100). The index's county-based measures range from Grant Parish, Louisiana, with a score of 16.05 and characterized as having a continuous low-density suburban development, to New York County, New York (Manhattan Island), with a score of 386.17 and characterized as having a high-density, mixed-use, highly centered development pattern with rich transportation options.

Key measures of maximizing land-use interactions relate to the ability to access land uses through multiple modes, especially those other than the single-occupant vehicle. Ewing and Hamidi (2014) apply their index to measure the relationship between compactness and transit use, walking, and overall travel times. I report Ewing et al.'s elasticities here.[4] What they found was that a 10 percent increase in the index score was significantly associated with the following percentage changes in these accessibility outcomes:

15.8 percent increase in the share of workers who take transit to work
7.6 percent increase in the share of workers who walk to work

3.1 percent decrease in driving time to work

To the extent that redevelopment increases land-use densities and intensities, mixed uses, centering, and street accessibility, land-use interactions would seem to be improved. I will include economic productivity outcomes in the quality of life discussion later.

## Fairly Distributing the Benefits of Development

The "public" part of a P3 should have a special concern about ensuring that the very development activities it uses public resources to facilitate benefit lower-income households. Favorable outcomes can be measured in at least three different ways with respect to using commercial corridor and node redevelopment: (1) providing opportunities to lower-income households, (2) improving accessibility to jobs, and (3) reducing housing plus transportation (H+T) costs.

The station area planning of the Dallas Area Rapid Transit Authority (DART) along commercial corridors and nodes is a good example of how these objectives are achieved. DART's light rail system began operating in 1996 and by 2013 had become the nation's largest light rail system. By design, its station areas facilitate infill and redevelopment along much of its eighty-five miles of lines.

Table 1.3 shows how the DART light rail system and associated redevelopment serve lower-income households. Within these corridors, median household income is less than the Dallas regional median, with proportionately about half of households earning the lowest income. Nearly 60 percent of the households along the DART system either do not own a vehicle or own just one vehicle compared with about 40 percent for the balance of the region. More important, about three times more households within a half mile of DART station areas use transit, walk, or bike to work than in the rest of region. Lastly, households within a half mile of DART station areas devote considerably less than half their incomes for housing plus transportation, while the balance of the region's households spend considerably more than half. It would seem that public investments

in transit and related corridor/node infrastructure improvements combined with advanced planning sensitive to private investment objectives
is fairly distributing the benefits of development.

**Table 1.3.**

DART Lower-Income Household Light Rail Outcomes Compared to the Dallas Region

| Metric | Within 0.5 Mile DART TOD | Balance of Dallas Region |
|---|---|---|
| *Household Income* | | |
| Total households | 70,236 | 2,084,896 |
| Median household income | $49,020 | $56,538 |
| Percent households under $25,000 | 29% | 20% |
| Percent households $25,000–$49,999 | 30% | 25% |
| Percent households $50,000–$74,999 | 17% | 19% |
| Percent households $75,000+ | 25% | 37% |
| *Job Accessibility* | | |
| Average travel time to work (minutes) | 23 | 27 |
| Percent who take public transportation | 5% | 1% |
| Percent who bicycle or walk | 4% | 2% |
| Percent transit, bicycle, or walk | 9% | 3% |
| Average vehicles per household | 1.5 | 1.8 |
| Percent households with 0 or 1 vehicle | 59% | 39% |
| *Housing + Transportation Costs* | | |
| H+T costs as percent of income | 44% | 53% |
| Housing costs as percent of income | 22% | 27% |
| Transportation costs as percent of income | 22% | 26% |

*Source*: Data adapted from the Center for Transit Oriented Development, http://toddata.
cnt.org/db_tool.php (accessed December 1, 2013).

## *Elevating the Quality of Life*

Quality of life as a concept can be elusive and more subjective than objective in measuring. On the other hand, Winnipeg, Canada, has developed a

comprehensive list of indicators and has generated data to measure them.[5] Quality of life includes such categories as urban environment, urban economy, community assets, individual well-being, and community governance. Common quality-of-life purposes of redevelopment include the following:

Enhancing the local economy
Stabilizing neighborhoods
Improving public safety and health

I applied the Ewing Compactness Index to estimate the elasticities of economic and housing performance outcomes over time. What I found was that a 10 percent increase in the index score was significantly associated with the following percentage changes in these economic and neighborhood stability outcomes:[6]

*Economic Outcomes*
1.0 percent increase in the mean ratio of gross regional product between 2000 and 2010 ($R^2 = 0.64$, $p > .01$), meaning that higher index scores are associated with more economic productivity over time.
0.6 percent increase in the mean ratio of jobs in 2010 compared to 2000 ($R^2 = 0.49$, $p > .01$), meaning that higher index scores are associated with more employment and implicitly lower unemployment rate over time (similar to findings of Ciccone and Hall 1996).

*Neighborhood Stability Outcomes*
19.3 percent decrease in the mean share of homes owned by banks between 2006 and 2011 ($R^2 = 0.80$, $p > .01$), meaning that higher index scores are associated with lower foreclosure rates over time and implicitly greater resilience to economic downturns.
2.8 percent increase in home values between 2000 and 2010 ($R^2 = 0.44$, $p > .01$), meaning that higher index scores are associated with higher home values and implicitly more home equity accumulation over time.

These outcomes to more compact, mixed-use, transportation-rich land-use patterns are not trivial. The mean Ewing Compactness Index score for all metropolitan counties is 100. A 10 percent increase nationally in the Ewing Compactness Index score (comparable to an increase from Fresno County, California, at 100 to Brazos County (San Antonio), Texas, at 110) would increase the nation's gross domestic product by about $130 billion annually and would increase employment by about 1 million jobs. Had the national Ewing Compactness Index been 110 in 2010, there may have been 1.5 million fewer homes for which foreclosure notices were filed than actually were filed (of 8.1 million).[7]

I also report public safety and health outcomes associated with the Ewing Compactness Index. For public safety, I report the elasticity of a 10 percent change in the index with respect to traffic and pedestrian facilities, and total crash rates, finding

1.0 percent fewer traffic fatalities,
1.9 percent fewer pedestrian facilities, and
0.5 percent fewer crashes.

For public health, I report the elasticity of a 10 percent change in the index with respect to the body mass index (BMI)—a measure of obesity and indirectly an indicator of more physical activity related to the urban form—finding

0.1 percent lower BMI.

A lower BMI translates into a longer life span, reduced days absent from work, and other favorable health outcomes (McCann and Ewing 2003).

As I found before, to the extent that redevelopment increases land-use densities and intensities, mixed uses, centering, and street accessibility, quality of life may be improved at least with respect to economic well-being, neighborhood stability, public safety focusing on traffic safety, and public health.

# Barriers to Optimal Redevelopment

There are several reasons why there is not more redevelopment. A key one is the gap between the rate of return developers need to justify these kinds of investments and what the market will generate. In many cases, developers need an average annual "unleveraged" rate of return of around 15 percent, though the range can be 10 percent (or lower) to 20 percent (or higher). "Unleveraged" means total project cost including debt financing and equity contributions (see chapter 3). The variation in rate of return targets reflects the risk developers assume—the higher the risk, the higher the return. A key role of the public sector is to reduce risk; in doing so, the rate of return can be reduced, making formerly infeasible projects feasible. Remedying the gap is what this book is about and will be the focus of later chapters. Here, first, I will review other barriers: antiquated planning and land-use controls, inadequate infrastructure, environmental constraints, parcel characteristics, legal/title/encumbrance conditions, not-in-my-backyard (NIMBY) opposition, and market limitations.[8]

## *Antiquated Planning and Land-Use Controls*

All too often, the principal barrier to making a redevelopment project financially feasible is antiquated zoning and land-use controls. While appropriate for a former time, development controls along commercial corridors and in employment centers are simply insensitive to redevelopment needs. Here, I review issues related to oversupply of a single use, infeasible maximum density/intensity, infeasible minimum density/intensity, excessive parking, preventing mixed uses, and inappropriate height limits.

*Oversupply of a single use.* Too many local governments overzone commercial corridors for office, retail, and other nonresidential land uses. Because the market can accommodate only so much supply, too much supply can depress land values. If other land uses are feasible but not allowed—such as apartments or senior living facilities—the local market is made less efficient. The local redevelopment should assess the realistic market demand for all land uses and then allocate sufficient supply to meet that demand but no more.

The result may be not only a better mix of development but also one that is more synergistic and adds long-term value to the community.

*Infeasible maximum density/intensity.* Market moves ahead of zoning and land-use controls in ways that make them barriers to redevelopment. If a light rail station is built in an area, residential zoning may be based on conditions prior to transit-oriented development (TOD). I know of situations where the underlying zoning restricted residential development to about twenty units per acre but the market would support three times that. So, even though the public TOD investment had been made, market investment did not follow. The solution is to raise density/intensity maxima to be consistent with market feasibility.

Often, in the case of residential development, all that is needed is an increase in zoning density. If the unleveraged rate of return of a project of twenty units per acre is 10 percent but the investors need 15 percent, maybe increasing the density to twenty-five units per acre will remedy the gap. Fregonese Associates did this simple analysis in south Los Angeles. The results show that increasing residential density along a commercial corridor leads to large-scale redevelopment and residential construction. Chapter 3 will demonstrate this.

*Infeasible minimum density/intensity.* At the other extreme is a local mindset that development should meet minimum expectations. I know of situations where land-use zoning around new light rail stations required minimum floor area ratios (FARs) that essentially require ten or more floor structures. The problem is the local market may not support such intensity for a few decades. In the meantime, the land is vacant or underused relative to current market conditions. One solution is to allow interim, lower-FAR development using wood-frame construction that may be relatively inexpensive to replace a few decades later. Such a strategy may actually accelerate conversion.

*Excessive parking.* Too many local land-use codes require more parking than is needed, either through excessive parking supply or by preventing efficient sharing of parking among different land uses (Willson 2013a). The result is lower private investment in economic development, lower property values, fewer jobs and economic transactions, and inefficient interaction between land uses (such as between office, retail, and residential uses that have staggered peak parking periods). Right-sizing parking can generate important economic, fiscal, and social benefits.

*Preventing mixed uses.* I am astonished by how inflexible zoning and land-use codes are around the nation, although this is changing. For instance, until a few years ago, the attitude among decision makers in Nashville was that the downtown was for only jobs and entertainment; people should not live downtown. But the downtown has been in a renaissance since residential development was allowed there. The same has happened to town squares where zoning allowed residential occupancy on upper floors and as infill development. Mixed land uses usually generate more economic development than homogeneous land uses.

There is another nuance. To encourage mixed-use development, some communities require two or more major uses within the same building, such as ground-floor retail and upper-floor residential. But desired development often does not occur, not because there is no market but because institutional lenders are wary. Pasadena, California, addressed this by encouraging single uses on individual parcels provided they were next to different uses, such as a residential building between a retail building and an office building.

*Inappropriate height limits.* Gone are the days when thirty-five feet was the limit for wood-frame construction, above which steel-frame construction was required by code. Engineered wood-frame construction supports structures up to fifty feet or more, especially if the main level is a steel/concrete podium. The result is much more intensive development at lower cost. The only impediment is whether the community does not have a fire ladder truck, in which case fire insurance rates may limit occupied floors to no higher than thirty-five feet.

What follows is a case study showing how a few changes to the zoning code facilitated redevelopment along a commercial corridor in Long Beach, California.

## Case Study: Zoning Changes in Long Beach, California, Lead to Redevelopment

In the late 2000s, Fregonese Associates worked with the City of Long Beach, California, on the potential for transit-oriented infill and redevelopment around the Metro Blue Line light rail stations along Long Beach Boulevard, which connects Long Beach to downtown Los Angeles. Although the boulevard was

**Figure 1.3.** Development along Long Beach Boulevard consistent with the City of Long Beach's zoning code in the 2000s. (Credit: Fregonese Associates)

once a major streetcar corridor, the rise of the automobile has changed the character of the corridor dramatically. Fregonese Associates analyzed the corridor for its potential as a revival of a TOD with mixed uses along an economically vital corridor.[9]

Existing parking standards and restrictive height limitations on significant portions of the corridor limited the feasibility of developing the kind of mixed-use developments the city wanted to have. Fregonese Associates found that if parking requirements were reduced to urban standards and the allowable height was increased from four to six stories (consistent with wood-frame construction standards), the market dynamics would tip in favor of mixed-use infill rather than single-story fast food chains and retail strip centers with large parking lots. The boulevard has been undergoing a transformation since these simple changes to the zoning code were made (see figs. 1.3 and 1.4).

As shown in each of these cases, existing plans and land-use codes are often easily fixed to facilitate redevelopment. Just what needs to be fixed and

**Figure 1.4.** Photomorph of the kind of development occurring along Long Beach Boulevard based on the revised zoning code since 2010. (Credit: Fregonese Associates)

how should be part of a redevelopment planning process that I present in chapter 2.

## Inadequate Infrastructure

Two key types of infrastructure are especially important to redevelopment: transportation and water-related utilities (water, wastewater, and drainage).

Inadequate access to sites can be in the form of dead-end streets or cul-de-sacs, inadequate sidewalks, street and intersection designs that inhibit street crossings, and other barriers to walking and driving. Successful redevelopment needs good connectivity between sites and to nearby neighborhoods. This may require increasing street connections or dividing large blocks during redevelopment, as well as requiring future street improvements to include sidewalks and bicycle lanes to increase connectivity. Moudon et al. (1997), for example, found that a very high share of all apartment complexes along commercial corridors in suburban Seattle, Washington, had no direct connectivity to retail opportunities that were often located on the adjacent parcel, so residents had no choice but to drive.

Infrastructure, especially water, sewer, and storm drainage, may need to be upgraded. This is a reason local governments commonly use to steer new commercial development farther out, because new infrastructure costs may be lower in greenfields than in redevelopment areas. This is false economics, however. Existing, aging infrastructure in developed urban areas needs to be upgraded at some point anyway, while new infrastructure farther out will also one day need to be upgraded. The long-term result may be to maintain and eventually replace two sets of infrastructure networks when in some situations only one may have been needed. Moreover, communities that fail to upgrade infrastructure will simply push development outward. The result is higher infrastructure costs as older systems are renewed while new ones are installed.

Given the vast amounts of existing structures that will need to be redeveloped, communities would be smart to upgrade existing inadequate infrastructure instead of building new infrastructure elsewhere. Indeed, the economic returns to "fix-it-first" programs in developed areas far exceed those of new infrastructure investments in greenfields (Department of the Treasury 2012).

### Environmental Constraints

Environmental barriers are often found on individual sites or in nearby areas. Developers are risk averse, so the prospect of assuming any environmental cleanup risk, even when the risks are small, may dissuade redevelopment. One role of the public sector is to take on those risks and to finance remediation, recouping costs through direct tax revenue from redevelopment combined with enhanced economic activity throughout the community. In some locations, habitat may need to be protected. The public sector should undertake a habitat survey to ascertain whether preservation measures are needed before attempting to facilitate redevelopment.

## Parcel Characteristics

The characteristics of the parcel itself indicate the extent to which redevelopment can occur efficiently. Based on a national survey, Greenstein and Sungu-Eryilmaz (2004) put some numbers to the factors that impede development of vacant land. Of the 186 responding cities (representing about 35 percent of all cities in the US), more than half noted that parcels were not large enough for development, about 40 percent noted that parcels were oddly shaped or in the wrong locations for development, and about a third indicated that other conditions—such as speculation, real or imagined contamination, steep slopes, wetlands, or infrastructure problems—prevented development. Using a land classification scheme developed by Northam (1971), Bowman and Pagano (2004) devised a typology of redevelopment probability, which is reported in table 1.4.[10] A key role of redevelopment is assembling land into buildable parcels and otherwise remedying development constraints.

**Table 1.4.**
Types of Urban Land for Redevelopment

| Type of Parcel | Site Characteristics | Probability of Redevelopment |
|---|---|---|
| Remnant land | Small size; irregular shape | Low: unsuitable for development |
| Land with physical limitations | Small or large; unbuildable due to slope, drainage, or other physical limitation | Low: unsuitable for development |
| Reserve parcels | Held by public, private, and nonprofit owners | High: eventual development likely |
| Speculative parcels | May be located in low-value or transitional areas; held in anticipation of increased future land values | High: especially in strong property markets; lower in weaker markets |
| Underdeveloped land | Existing land-use intensity (floor area ratio) and/or density well below potential | High: eventual development likely |
| Derelict land | Damaged parcels; brownfields that are contaminated or perceived to be contaminated | Low: unless the parcel is restored to an acceptable standard for development |

*Source:* Adapted from Greenstein and Sungu-Eryilmaz (2004). The underdeveloped land example has been added.

## Legal/Title/Encumbrance Conditions

Even where other barriers have been removed, there can be legal, title, and encumbrance issues that prevent redevelopment from occurring. There also might not be a clear title even if the ostensible owner of the parcel wants to participate. Easements, covenants, conditions, and other forms of encumbrances can limit how the property is developed and used. A key role of the public sector is to resolve these issues, sometimes exercising eminent domain as a last resort. In many states, public acquisition of private property—whether through negotiation or through eminent domain—results in extinguishing title and encumbrance barriers.

## NIMBY Opposition

Residential neighbors may become involved in a project, often as opponents to change near their homes. In *The Homevoter Hypothesis*, William Fischel (2001) explains NIMBY behavior as a rational response to change. Homeowners, who are also "voters," have much of their wealth invested in homes, so they will logically do anything needed to preserve the value of those homes. Fischel observes that the greatest fear of NIMBYs is losing value. They will even oppose development that promises to increase value, perhaps from fear of being misled.

More often, the outcome of development or redevelopment is not lower but higher value. But NIMBY interests may also be concerned that successful development will raise their property values and thus their property taxes. For some, they could see having to move out of the area because of their inability to pay the higher property taxes. In my view, there is one solution to this for some people, while for others some accommodation may be enabled by state legislatures. Most states already allow seniors to defer their property taxes until they sell their homes. While many seniors see this as reducing the value of their estate, it is nonetheless an option that does not push seniors out of their homes prematurely because of property taxes. For others, a solution could be similar wherein property values for homes within a certain distance or redevelopment would be frozen based on some formula, but once the property sold it would be revalued for tax purposes at the higher level. Or, perhaps owners of property within a certain distance of redevelopment could apply for deferred property taxes based on the difference between the higher value after redevelopment and a floor based on pre-redevelopment value.[11]

A large share of NIMBY opposition to redevelopment is a result of ineffective planning and planning communication. For one thing, most urban redevelopment occurs on existing nonresidential parcels. Nonresidential development occupies about a third of the built environment but nearly all of the land along commercial corridors and suburban centers and most of downtowns. Redevelopment thus occurs substantially on already-developed land that is dedicated to uses other than residential. Effective redevelopment planning needs neighbors who are motivated to simultaneously deflect development pressure away from their neighborhoods and direct it into aging commercial sites, especially if they have a constructive say in how they are redeveloped. I discuss this in the next chapter.

## Market Barriers

Of the many potential market barriers, I will focus on three here: land price, lack of developer interest, and unpredictable mixed-use timing.

*Land price.* When a redevelopment plan is adopted, nondeveloper property owners may have excessive expectations of value that can discourage private real estate investment. Over time, they may moderate their expectations, but by then the market may have moved on to other locations, including less efficient ones. One public sector approach may be to adopt the plan but to require case-by-case rezoning to implement it. Such a scheme would induce the property owner to partner with the developer to unlock a reasonable value of the land.[12] Another approach may be to "sunset" the plan after a few years to encourage landowners to sell their property lest a new plan reduce development prospects.[13] A more pragmatic approach may be to engage property owners with prospective developers so that communication about market opportunities and expected values can be broached from the beginning. Of course, the last resort may be for the public entity to exercise powers of eminent domain to implement the public-purpose elements of approved plans, though in many states these powers are highly restricted.

*Lack of developer interest.* Many developers do not have the means to conduct their own market studies or identify particular market niches that make sense to them.

The redevelopment process may also seem daunting, and for many it is simpler to look for easier development opportunities elsewhere, including the suburban fringe. One solution may be a proactive public development agency (PDA) that conducts market analyses on behalf of prospective developers and then works with them closely through the entitlement, permitting, and financing processes. The PDA itself may not be a financial partner, but in many other respects it has a partnership-like role. Indeed, many successful infill/redevelopment developers are successful because they have a partner in the public sector that facilitates meeting development requirements.

*Unpredictable mixed-use timing.* Although future prospects for development may appear strong, achieving long-term outcomes can be challenging. For instance, there may be long-term demand for residential and retail development for an area but without one the other may not occur. A public sector role may be to leverage the private sector in one or more mixed-use activities in the short term, allowing them to become established and mutually beneficial over a reasonable period.

One or often more of these barriers may prevent optimal redevelopment of a site or area. But neither the public nor private sector alone can overcome most of them. P3s are needed to identify the barriers and how to overcome them to facilitate redevelopment.

## Case Study: Atlanta Inner City Redevelopment

As in many cities, large areas near downtown Atlanta had been abandoned or underdeveloped for several decades. The planning and zoning for these areas was antiquated, infrastructure needed upgrading, ownerships were in small parcels and often with unclear title, and, while neighbors favored redevelopment, they were also wary.

During the 1990s, the City of Atlanta, Georgia, went through the statutory process of designating many of these areas as blighted; worked with neighborhood groups and other community stakeholders to prepare redevelopment plans; updated development codes; borrowed money by selling tax allocation district (TAD) bonds through Georgia's TAD process (known as tax increment financing, or TIF, elsewhere); upgraded infrastructure; acquired and prepared land for development; added public amenities, such as parks and pathways; built parking garages; and in some cases added public indoor spaces in targeted redevelopment areas. Through P3 development agreements, the redeveloped areas saw the construction of

more than nine thousand new residential units, with more than two thousand of them affordable;

more than five million square feet of office and retail spaces;

nearly one thousand hotel rooms; and

nearly twenty-eight thousand square feet of parking structure spaces.

In addition, tax abatement was used to reduce property taxes on owner-occupied condominium units at the rate of 100 percent in the first year and declining by 10 percent annually to the tenth year. About $370 million in public investment leveraged nearly $3.3 billion in private investment, with a total market value in 2013 of more than $4 billion.[14]

In table 1.5, I estimate that new development generates about $74 million in average annual property and sales tax revenues. The incremental property tax revenues are sufficient to retire the TAD bonds in about a dozen years. A reasonable balance is also achieved between the new residential units and the jobs created in the area. I estimate that these TAD redevelopment projects generated about fifteen thousand jobs, resulting in a jobs–housing ratio of 1.64 compared to the Atlanta metropolitan area average of 1.53. What this means is that many people living in these redevelopment projects can also work there.

**Table 1.5.**
Atlanta Leveraged Development Metrics

| Metric | Figure |
|---|---|
| Estimated annual sales and property taxes (millions) | $74.0 |
| Estimated property tax break-even years | 12 |
| Residential units | 9,320 |
| Affordable residential units | 2,207 |
| Estimated residents | 25,936 |
| Estimated jobs | 15,263 |
| Jobs–housing balance | 1.64 |
| Atlanta metropolitan area | 1.53 |

*Source*: Central Atlanta Progress.
*Note:* Estimates by the author.

There are, in fact, several TAD areas, but two are the most relevant here: the Westside and Eastside Tax Allocation Districts.

A joint venture among the City of Atlanta, Fulton County, and the Atlanta School Board was formed in 1998 to create the Westside Tax Allocation District, managed by the Atlanta Redevelopment Authority (ADA). The Westside TAD covers 1,451 acres. It includes historically black neighborhoods; parts of downtown comprising Centennial Olympic Park (built for the 1996 Olympics); and the South Central Business District (CBD), the emerging downtown arts district, a railroad gulch, and a former warehousing district. Since the 1970s, the area had been experiencing disinvestment and stagnating real estate investment despite the metropolitan Atlanta area more than doubling in population. It was also an area of high unemployment and crime rates. Yet, it is well positioned to provide much of the city's redevelopment opportunities over the next several decades. Given its conditions and opportunities, tax allocation financing is used to leverage developments that advance the following four goals.[15]

*Transportation improvements* that enhance connectivity between the area and the CBD, Georgia Tech, Atlanta University, and adjacent neighborhoods; provide parking and pedestrian improvements to support P3 development; and maximize access to public transit.

*Community development*, including improving quality of life; completing tourist-related facilities; enhancing public parks and plazas; and increasing public safety, among other objectives.

*Economic growth* through overcoming impediments to development and increasing investment in the area; increasing the tax base; assembling land and air rights for redevelopment; increasing jobs; and enticing P3 investments through enhancements to streetscaping, streets and sewers, and greenway trails.

*Land-use interactions* through public, private, market rate, affordable, and senior housing; commercial, residential, retail, and entertainment mixed uses; retail, schools, childcare, public safety facilities, and related community services; and hotels, corporate offices and headquarters, and art/cultural and related facilities.

The Eastside Tax Allocation District was formed by the same partners in 2003 and is also managed by the ADA. The Eastside TAD comprises about

890 acres. It promotes commercial and residential development in downtown Atlanta by facilitating the formation of P3s to leverage real estate investment to create jobs and housing in a "24-hour" downtown. It is also intended to leverage revitalization of the historically black Auburn Avenue corridor and the Memorial Drive/Martin Luther King Jr. Drive corridor

While TAD financing is the principal means of leveraging private investment, other tools are also used, including tax abatement, small business loans, new markets tax credits, and other bond programs.[16] In addition, because both TADs included several large brownfields, federal and state brownfield remediation resources are available.

In all, through the early 2010s, the TAD programs facilitated more than fifty development and redevelopment projects, some as small as less than one acre to others of more than forty acres; most ranged between one and ten acres, however.

Consider how these outcomes relate to the redevelopment goals I posed earlier. Public goods in the form of reduced land consumption have been achieved, and in fact former brownfields have been converted into productive real estate projects. The costs of public facilities have been minimized by upgrading existing infrastructure that would have to be upgraded anyway but without adding new infrastructure elsewhere to accommodate development needs. Maximizing land-use interactions has been achieved through mixed-use development, with all projects accessible to public transit. The benefits of redevelopment are to lower income households through the provision of affordable housing (equivalent to about a quarter of all units built) and by creating a favorable jobs–housing balance. Given the characteristics of these developments—higher density and intensity, substantially mixed uses, location at or near centers, and improved street accessibility—quality of life would also seem to be improved based on insights from the Ewing Compactness Index.

In chapter 2, I will present more details on the redevelopment planning process and its implementation through public-private partnerships.

# Chapter 2

# Implementation of Redevelopment Plans and the Role of Public-Private Partnerships

We have entered into a period of the nation's history when there may be more redevelopment of the built environment than development of greenfields. Redevelopment is vastly more complex, however, as I will show in later chapters. The future of real estate redevelopment will require more partnerships between the public and the private sectors, with each relying on the other to contribute what it does best.

This book is about the role of public-private partnerships in facilitating the infill and redevelopment of the existing built landscape. P3s are often a contractual relationship between public sector agencies and private sector interests. The first step in the process is to justify the public role in redevelopment; otherwise, public resources cannot be used for this purpose. The next step is to prepare the redevelopment plan.

From a planning and public policy perspective, the primary function of P3s is to implement the redevelopment plans to broadly achieve their public purposes. The plans guide public sector efforts to leverage private real estate development to achieve certain outcomes within specific planning areas. They may also be known as sector plans or special area plans. The plans should be based on analysis showing that an area has important community and economic development opportunities that can be achieved through redevelopment, rehabilitation/repurposing of existing structures, historic preservation, or other kinds of development in the area. They also need to address the public health, safety, or welfare benefits of redevelopment. In some states, it may be useful to identify areas that are blighted or may become blighted but for the plan and implementing policies.

Redevelopment plans are often implemented by special government agencies designed for this purpose. They are typically called development or redevelopment authorities or agencies. In this book, I will call them collectively public development authorities (or PDAs), though they can go by many other names. PDAs often have special statutory powers for entering into agreements, borrowing and spending money, acquiring and preparing land for development, and other activities.

A key role of PDAs is to leverage private real estate investment to help implement the objectives of the redevelopment plan. This is done through development agreements, which are contracts between the PDA and a private real estate development interest. Development agreements often specify how each partner benefits. For the private entity, benefits could include agreement on the scale, design, phasing, and other development conditions; they may also include exemptions from future land-use changes if they prevent implementation of the agreement within a certain period. The agreement may also specify how the public benefits, such as including certain design features that mitigate adverse impacts; how the developed property may be used, including the number of workers to be employed; and any payments the development will need to pay the public agency and the conditions under which such payments would occur. I introduce more details on how development agreements are structured below.

An important resource available to PDAs may be patient equity contributions to P3s. These contributions leverage private real estate investment, and local governments often provide financial incentives in the form of grants, fee waivers, property tax abatement, and low interest loans, among others (see chapter 4 for a review). Christopher Leinberger advocates converting these financial concessions into a form of equity stake in P3 deals. Over time, as a project matures and generates higher rates of return, the public sector is rewarded through a share of the returns (see chapter 4 for details on how this works). Because the public sector does not have the immediacy of returns that the private sector has, its equity contribution is "patient."

I will now outline the key elements of the redevelopment planning process and implementation through P3s. Basic steps include justifying the role of the public in facilitating redevelopment, elements of the redevelopment, the basic structure of development agreements as a key part of a public-private partnership, and principles of successful P3s.

## Justifying the Public Role in Redevelopment

The public role in redevelopment in the United States is rooted in the history of city planning. A report to the National Association of Realtors by the law firm Robinson and Cole (2007) provides a historic perspective combined with a review of redevelopment statutes in all states and the District of Columbia. This section is based largely on Robinson and Cole's report.[1]

Most state legislatures have enacted statutes guiding public agencies to redevelop "blighted" areas. Declaring that an area is blighted is essential before private property is condemned and acquired by public agencies for redevelopment by public or private interests. The concept of blight and the necessity for its removal stems from early twentieth-century efforts to eradicate slums. The slum clearance movement was based on the assumption that housing quality affected the health and social interactions of residents. Only by removing slums could high-quality housing be provided, thereby improving public health and social interactions. The urban renewal movement thus had its origins in removing slums.

By the 1920s, the urban planning movement had evolved to combine zoning and comprehensive planning to facilitate urban renewal. The Model Planning and Zoning Enabling Acts, advanced by then secretary of commerce Herbert Hoover, gave federal guidance to local efforts to develop comprehensive plans implemented by zoning for the purpose of separating land uses and redeveloping underdeveloped parts of communities.

The urban renewal movement objected to blight for three key reasons: (1) it harmed residents and drained urban resources by requiring increased use of public resources for social services and police services, (2) it undermined economic growth and inhibited the evolution of modern cities, and (3) it led to unproductive and socially harmful slums.

How to prevent slums from rising in blighted areas and, more directly, how to redevelop blighted areas became a growing public policy question. In the 1930s, the Urban Land Institute (ULI) posed the idea that a private redevelopment agency could condemn property, clear and improve the land for redevelopment, and then convey it to private developers for redevelopment, all provided three-quarters of the property owners in an area agreed. Although largely unworkable, the idea of a public agency stepping in to perform these functions (without a vote of affected property owners) gained traction so that by 1948 more than half the states had laws enabling this scheme.

In part to make cities attractive to private investment, Congress passed the Housing Act of 1949, which included an "urban renewal" program. The act provided federal funding to cover the cost of acquiring "slums" as defined in the act. Costs included razing structures, combining land ownerships into larger, more efficiently developable sites, and improving infrastructure. Ultimately, the sites were sold or otherwise transferred to private developers for redevelopment. Later, the 1954 Housing Act provided mortgages backed by the Federal Housing Administration to facilitate housing redevelopment. In general, criteria for declaring an area blighted require the following:

- It is a qualified census tract or an area of chronic economic distress.
- It is an area established within a municipality that has a substantial number of substandard, slum, deteriorated, or deteriorating structures and it suffers from a relatively high rate of unemployment.

Now, all states and the District of Columbia have statutes enabling public-private partnerships for redevelopment. Needless to say, individual states vary widely in how they target areas for redevelopment and frame the role of the public sector in facilitating private redevelopment of those areas. Robinson and Cole group statutes into three themes that guide local redevelopment efforts: (1) the selection of properties to be developed, (2) the causes of blight, and (3) the consequences of blight.

They start with five approaches used in the selection of properties to be redeveloped:

- There should not be any property selection factors, meaning there is no need for maps or other documents specifying which properties are subject to public participation in redevelopment.
- Properties are located within a specified area.
- Areas eligible for blight designation include (1) structures, buildings, or other improvements; and/or (2) a majority of the properties or

structures are determined to be blighted; and/or (3) a majority of the properties are to be used for residential purposes (though not necessarily for lower-income households).

- Single properties may be eligible for blight designation.
- Unique selection factors need to be considered such as requirements that an area must meet certain federal statutory requirements or that an area must be predominantly open or of a certain size.

They continue with four sets of factors used to characterize blight:

- Public health, safety, and welfare causes, such as (1) health hazards relating to buildings that are not current with modern building standards and codes or that contain hazardous materials or are infested with insects, rodents, or diseases; (2) fire hazards; (3) structural defects; (4) declared disaster areas; (5) physical/geological defects; and/or (6) the age of structures;
- Factors relating to how the land is used, such as (1) overcrowding and/or excessive land coverage; (2) faulty/obsolete planning; (3) neighborhood character relating to nonconforming uses or accepted levels of density based on the adequate provision of open space, light, air, and public infrastructure; (4) blighted open areas, in particular vacant lots amid deteriorating buildings; (5) traffic congestion; and/or (6) areas that require expensive levels of public services and/or that lack sufficient amenities and utilities
- Economic vitality factors relating to (1) the best economic use of land where the objective is to determine the most economically productive use of the land and to declare as blighted those properties that fail to meet that standard; (2) high vacancy rates; and/or (3) unpaid property taxes that would lead the public sector to acquire such properties through tax foreclosures
- Ownership factors, including (1) diversity of ownerships, such as when multiple parcels are held by different owners, or single parcels are held by multiple owners, or determination of ownership is not possible; and/or (2) uncertain or unclear title.

Robinson and Cole note there are these significant consequences of blight:

- Comprising public health, safety, welfare, and moral conditions such as ill health or crime, perhaps resulting from concentrated poverty, crime, and/or insufficient social services combined with vacant lots, overcrowding, and/or mixing of inappropriate land uses
- Lagging economic investment manifested as (1) lack of investment in the commercial, institutional, and/or residential sectors, perhaps because of high crime and unemployment rates; and/or (2) lagging economic growth as measured by high or increasing vacancy rates, decreasing employment opportunities, or declining retail activity
- Lagging housing investment manifested as (1) a lack of adequate amounts of affordable housing through such activities as conversions of apartments and offices to condominiums; or (2) buildings that are structurally unsound, thereby preventing safe occupancy.

Robinson and Cole observe that every state and the District of Columbia require one or more "cause factors" to be present before an area is designated as blighted. In some states, a "blight finding" can apply to a single parcel of land in need of remediation. Other states allow a public agency to designate an entire area as blighted even if not all properties themselves are considered blighted. Although states vary in the number of cause factors that are used—from at least one to many—I like Kansas's Development and Redevelopment of Areas in and Around Cities statute because it illustrates the wide range of cause factors that can be considered individually or collectively. The Kansas statute defines a "blighted area" as follows (somewhat paraphrased):[2]

*(1) Because of the presence of a majority of the following factors, a "blighted area" substantially impairs or arrests the development and growth of the municipality or constitutes an economic or social liability or is a menace to the public health, safety, morals or welfare in its present condition and use: (a) a substantial number of deteriorated or deteriorating structures; (b) predominance of defective or inadequate street layout; (c) unsanitary or unsafe conditions; (d) deterioration of site improvements; (e) tax or special assessment delinquency exceeding the fair market value of the real property; (f) defective or unusual*

*conditions of title including but not limited to cloudy or defective titles, multiple or unknown ownership interests to the property; (g) improper subdivision or obsolete platting or land uses; (h) the existence of conditions which endanger life or property by fire or other causes; or (i) conditions which create economic obsolescence; or (2) has been identified by any state or federal environmental agency as being environmentally contaminated to an extent that requires a remedial investigation.*

Once statutory criteria have been met, redevelopment planning and implementation may proceed as guided by a government agency. It is the *planning* part that I address next.

## The Redevelopment Plan

Here, I discuss the role of a redevelopment plan, which guides public sector efforts to leverage private real estate redevelopment. The redevelopment planning process begins by identifying the area to be redeveloped. It should be based on analysis showing the area has important community and economic development opportunities through redevelopment, which can include rehabilitation, conservation (such as historic preservation), or development of the area. To be consistent with planning, the analysis should also identify the public health, safety, or welfare benefits of redevelopment. In some states, it may be useful to identify areas that are blighted or that may become blighted but for the plan and implementing policies.

During the analysis stage, there should be an assessment of all land uses, focusing on their current stage of occupancy; market value; land-use patterns; infrastructure capacity, including the extent to which there is deferred maintenance; building conditions, including identifying those that have serious code violations; ownership patterns; assessment of environmental conditions, such as drainage and brownfield conditions; and the extent to which individual buildings are approaching if not exceeding their economic or functional use. There are probably hundreds if not thousands of good redevelopment plans around the United States. For my purposes here, the plan developed by Hillsboro, Oregon, is instructive (City of Hillsboro 2010). Hillsboro made the following findings justifying the need for a redevelopment plan (which it calls an urban renewal plan):

> Structures obsolete for contemporary commercial and industrial uses due to inadequate interior arrangement or size
> Economic disuse of property
> Some platted properties and lots that prevent efficient use or redevelopment in accordance with local land-use policies
> Inadequate transportation facilities, parks, open spaces, and utilities
> Underutilized commercial, industrial, and mixed-use properties
> Decreasing level of investment/improvements in some areas
> Housing insufficient to support employees, businesses, and other economic development initiatives of downtown

It is important to note that many redevelopment laws were written to favor large developers over small landowners and existing residents. In the past, redevelopment plans used statutory criteria to designate areas as blighted even though they were functional, socially cohesive, economically sustainable neighborhoods composed of a mix of uses, property ownership spread among many people, and with human- as opposed to automobile-scaled streets.

All plans, especially redevelopment plans, need to have overall goals. Hillsboro's goals include the following:[3]

> Strengthening and sustaining community
> Enhancing neighborhoods and districts
> Preserving the environment
> Creating economic opportunity
> Expanding educational and cultural horizons
> Promoting health and safety

In my view, most redevelopment will be small scale and will occur on a parcel-by-parcel basis. The reason is simple: more than 85 percent of all commercial buildings in the United States are owned by private investors, about 90 percent of all commercial structures are one (67 percent) or two (22 percent) floors, and more than 95 percent of all structures are less than fifty thousand square feet in size.[4] They also sit on individual parcels and have different periods during which they become ripe for redevelopment (presented later in this section). Hillsboro's plan is designed to facilitate small-scale redevelopment, which is why I highlight it in this book. The case study in chapter 4 is, in fact, a 1.1-acre redevelopment site in Hillsboro.

After establishing the redevelopment planning area, the local government needs to prepare the plan. This can be done efficiently with a mix of public officials, consultants, and community stakeholders. One of the first things the plan needs is an overall assessment of market opportunities and how current conditions in the redevelopment area are barriers. What kinds of jobs and households would be attracted to an area given its location, features, and amenities? For instance, in *Reshaping Metropolitan America* (Nelson 2013b), I estimated that for most metropolitan areas, all the new demand for housing and jobs could occur in existing developed downtowns, areas near downtowns, commercial corridors, and suburban centers that have transit options (notably light rail, street cars, and bus rapid transit)—with most of the demand in existing developed suburban areas. The reason is that roughly one-quarter to one-third of Americans want transit accessibility, and a third or more of firms want this as well. Even if all new development to 2030 occurred in these locations, demand would still not be met.

The plan should also have provisions for land assembly, managing redevelopment processes, financing infrastructure upgrades, and identifying ways to leverage private real estate investment for redevelopment. Chapter 4 reviews categories of leveraging tools.

The Hillsboro plan is again instructive by including these elements, which are distilled and paraphrased here from the original:

- Offering financial assistance for rehabilitation, preservation, development, or redevelopment through grants and market or below-market loans
- Providing property owners with technical assistance in the form of site, market, and feasibility studies; predevelopment analyses; engineering, planning, and design activities; and assessments of energy efficiency and historic preservation

- Using loans or grants to make improvements to the exterior, street-facing portion of structures and sites
- Improving transportation flow, transit access, and parking, as well as providing street trees and landscaping, pedestrian and bicycle facilities, curb extensions, traffic-calming enhancements, street lighting, street furniture, public art, way-finding signage, historic markers/signage, and related activities
- Improving and, where needed, upgrading utilities, including using tax increment financing or other forms of local improvement districts to help finance them
- Providing financial and technical assistance to encourage rehabilitation and preservation of the existing housing stock and development or redevelopment of new housing complementary to the area, including grants, market or below-market loans, or technical assistance in the form of feasibility studies; market analyses; engineering, planning, and design activities; and assessments of energy efficiency and historic preservation.

The plan will need to go through a public review and a hearing process. Once these are completed, the local governing body should formally adopt the redevelopment plan, including amending its current planning, zoning, and land-use control codes as needed.

Three other important technical elements should also be included in the planning process: identifying market opportunities, mapping and evaluating redevelopment opportunities, and creating the opportunity for successional development that seizes short-term development opportunities which are consistent with the long-term scenario.

## Identifying Market Opportunities

Planners need to identify future development needs, inventory current development conditions, and assess opportunities for meeting future needs given current conditions and emerging trends.

For instance, housing needs between 2010 and 2040 in the United States will be far different from those of the period 1980 to 2010. The latter period was when baby boomers were in the peak of their earning power and also had growing families that needed space; thus, they dominated the residential market, and communities largely met their needs. In the thirty years following that period, those same boomers will have become empty nesters while millions will also have lost their partners, and they will be downsizing into smaller homes, including attached options. The generations following them will likely have less purchasing power than boomers, which in turn will affect their housing options.

The nonresidential market will also change dramatically. During their peak income and housing need period, boomers reshaped the retail market and, along with high technology, recast entire economic sectors. Those same boomers will demand social assistance and medical care in unprecedented numbers, so while they will require fewer retail services, they will need more medical and personal services. To a substantial extent, it will be the younger generations that will cater to the needs of the boomers.

In addition, the nonresidential demand for central urban and suburban locations with transit options seems certain to increase (Nelson 2013a).

Because emerging markets are very different from what the current built landscape provides, communities will need to acquire highly informed projections of future housing and nonresidential needs. These needs should be characterized in terms of preferred locations (such as downtowns, near downtowns, commercial corridors, and suburban centers), whether and what kind of transit is needed, what land and building space are needed, the extent to which being in mixed-use development is desired, and related factors. The future needs should be compared to existing conditions to show the difference between them. For instance, if market analysis shows the opportunity for a mix of jobs and housing in a redevelopment area that will need one hundred thousand gallons of water per day in, say, 2040, but the current water supply system can provide only half that, the gap will need to be remedied if redevelopment is to be successful.

On the other hand, many potential redevelopment areas enjoy excess capacity in key public facilities. In chapter 1, I showed that substantial excess capacity exists in Albuquerque's infill/redevelopment area to accommodate new development for several decades at a fraction of the cost of accommodating new development in greenfield areas. Determining future needs and comparing them to current conditions will provide a road map for planning.

## Mapping and Analyzing Redevelopment Opportunities

Redevelopment plans should evaluate the nature of current development and estimate the optimal time of redevelopment. I have pioneered a method that is transparent and easily applied.

The method determines when parcels become available for development in different time periods, based on comparing land and building value. I define the optimal time for redevelopment to occur when the market value of land exceeds the depreciated replacement value of the structure. All structures depreciate and eventually have to be rebuilt or replaced. (Appendix B lists major structure types and their estimated depreciation rates.) On the other hand, land value increases by roughly the rate of growth (adjusting for inflation). In growing areas, the optimal time for redevelopment can occur well before the structure is fully depreciated. In chapter 1, I showed that a fifty-year structure on a parcel of land that appreciated 2 percent per year becomes an opportunity for development at about the thirtieth year, although the optimal time for redevelopment would be a few years before or after. Although the actual optimal timing for redevelopment depends on other factors I reviewed in chapter 1, this approach is nonetheless an objective, transparent, and measurable indicator. To estimate the optimal timing of redevelopment for any given parcel, five pieces of data are needed:[5]

Base year
Base year land value
Population growth rate (average annual)
Base year structure value
Structure depreciation period (years)

Each year, the land value increases by the average annual projected population growth rate, while the building value depreciates based on the structure depreciation period. Table 2.1 illustrates these calculation steps.

**Table 2.1.**
Estimating Optimal Timing of Redevelopment

| Figure | Variable |
|---|---|
| 2015 | Base year |
| $1,000,000 | Base year land value |
| 2.0% | Population growth rate (average annual) |
| $2,000,000 | Base year structure value |
| 50 | Structure depreciation period (years) |
| 17 | Years to optimal redevelopment |
| 2032 | Year of optimal redevelopment |
| 2027–2037 | Optimal year of redevelopment ± 5 years |

*Note:* Years to optimal redevelopment calculated as:
(base year structure value–base year land value) /
[(base year land value × population growth rate) +
(base year structure value × structure depreciation period)]

The approach assumes that the demand for buildable land will increase faster than its supply, which will increase the value of land over time. For simplicity, I assume that the rate of increase in land value will be equivalent to the rate of population increase. Demand for urban land is a function not only of population growth but also of demand for employment, retail, and other land uses. Thus, the demand for urban land grows faster than population, and using the population growth rate as the increase in land value represents a conservative estimate. The model can be refined, such as by including more precise information on depreciation and using compounded instead of average annual growth rates, but these improvements usually result in only small changes to the outcome the simpler method generates. I also recommend including a five-year before-and-after band around the optimal redevelopment timing year to indicate a range.

The building cost to land ratio varies by building type. Newly built single-family homes typically have a three- or four-to-one building to land ratio, while newly constructed high-rise office buildings may have a building to land ratio greater than twenty-to-one. The method relies on local property tax assessor data, so if those data have little resemblance to actual market value, this source of data may not be useful.

Each class of building needs to be assigned a depreciation period. Marshall and Swift, for instance, provide these for hundreds of building types based

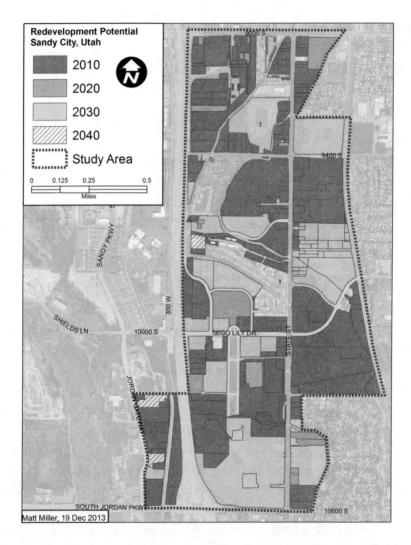

**Figure 2.1.** Redevelopment timing opportunities for Sandy, Utah, in ten-year increments, 2010–2040, where 2010, for example, means land value exceeds improvement value in 2010. (In the public domain; created by Matt Miller, University of Utah)

on several construction quality indicators.[6] I have simplified their data in appendix B, using their average construction quality rating for the range of land uses typically included in assessor records. This approach will underestimate the optimal year of redevelopment for some structures and will overestimate it for others. The point is to generate a general range of redevelopment opportunity timing.

Actual building value tends to fluctuate over the life span of the building rather than following a linear pattern. Most buildings have ongoing repairs and maintenance during the course of normal use, which serve to restore some building value. It is important to recognize that repairs and maintenance do not restore the building to its original state and thus do not restore full value. Although the actual percentage of original value depends on the quality of the repair, a patch is never as good as the whole material. Second, the degree of value restored by repairs also declines with time. Ad hoc repairs impair the ability to make further repairs. Finally, the quality of repairs tends to decline as the building depreciates. Over a longer time scale, the more durable parts of a building require replacement as well. The cumulative effect of wind and weather over decades may not be obvious in any given year, but they manifest in the increasing need for repairs and maintenance as more parts of the building reach the end of their useful livelihood and need to be replaced. At some point, the expected costs of continued maintenance exceed the value of the building, and the building is no longer worth maintaining—the building value has fallen to zero.

The redevelopment plan should apply this or a similar method to map the optimal redevelopment range of years for each parcel in the redevelopment area. This is illustrated in figure 2.1 for Sandy, Utah. The figure shows ten-year time frames within which each nonresidential (or mixed-use residential and nonresidential) parcel will become an opportunity for redevelopment. The darker shades show development opportunities in the earlier years (2010 in this case), while lighter shades show opportunities by parcel to 2040. Because Sandy may wish to preserve existing residential structures, they were excluded from this analysis but could easily have been added. Also excluded were historically significant structures. The map thus shows just those parcels on which the city may wish to focus redevelopment efforts.

Table 2.2 summarizes analysis for ten-year periods from 2010 to 2040. In 2010, more than half the land area (63 percent) and about a fifth of the structure space were already redevelopment opportunities because land value exceeded improvement value. By 2020 and beyond, virtually all of the parcels included in the analysis would become opportunities for redevelopment. Sandy was

**Table 2.2.**
Optimal Redevelopment Opportunities by Ten-Year Period

| Land Uses | Total 2010 | Redevelopment Opportunity 2010 | Redevelopment Opportunity 2010–2020 | Redevelopment Opportunity 2020–2030 | Redevelopment Opportunity 2030–2040 |
|---|---|---|---|---|---|
| **Institutional** | | | | | |
| Square feet | 1,348 | 0 | 1,012 | 332 | 4 |
| Acres | 151 | 0 | 108 | 15 | 15 |
| **Industrial** | | | | | |
| Square feet | 985 | 985 | 985 | 985 | 985 |
| Acres | 39 | 39 | 39 | 39 | 39 |
| **Mixed Use** | | | | | |
| Square feet | 84 | 82 | 1 | — | — |
| Acres | 5 | 5 | 0 | — | — |
| **Office** | | | | | |
| Square feet | 9,825 | 478 | 789 | 6,426 | 2,132 |
| Acres | 69 | 7 | 4 | 53 | 5 |
| **Service/ Entertainment** | | | | | |
| Square feet | 1,830 | 1,154 | 1,730 | 301 | 1,355 |
| Acres | 47 | 39 | 17 | 2 | 12 |
| **Warehouse** | | | | | |
| Square feet | 298 | 259 | 39 | — | — |
| Acres | 16 | 14 | 3 | — | — |
| **Retail** | | | | | |
| Square feet | 18,132 | 9,677 | 2,822 | 5,633 | 0 |
| Acres | 251 | 138 | 12 | 101 | 0 |
| **Vacant** | | | | | |
| Square feet | 142 | 142 | — | — | — |
| Acres | 96 | 96 | — | — | — |
| **Total** | | | | | |
| Square feet | 33,998 | 12,777 | 5,339 | 13,444 | 2,437 |
| Share 2010 | 100% | 38% | 16% | 40% | 7% |
| Acres | 687 | 463 | 39 | 177 | 8 |
| Share 2010 | 100% | 67% | 6% | 26% | 1% |

strategic in analyzing this particular area when it did, because through its planning and P3 efforts, much of it will be redeveloped by the end of the 2020s.

## Planning for Successional Development

Planners often want to design plans to achieve an idealized build-out scheme for a redevelopment area. These can take the form of minimum floor area ratio (FAR) intensities, minimum residential densities, and certain urban design and building form requirements, among others. Build-out plans can also include attractive artist renderings of what the area may look like. While the ultimate development of an area may assume the intended composition and form, however, those expectations may be ahead of the market by years or decades. In the meantime, nothing happens, so little is gained in stimulating development and economic activity through a redevelopment plan.

The solution may be allowing for *successional development* so that financially feasible real estate investment occurs as an interim activity before the market catches up to the build-out scheme. The public sector would thus need to accept low-quality, low-rise development in the near term but create mechanisms that allow efficient conversion of interim development to build out when market conditions warrant. These measures may include identifying future street extensions configured so that new street improvements can be constructed concurrent with the future development envisioned in the redevelopment plan; this may also include placing interim structures away from future street extensions to preserve the option to make road improvements even before interim development gives way to the envisioned development. They may also include sizing and providing some infrastructure improvements where envisioned future development is desired; doing so can allow public investments to be leveraged as interim development and become opportunities for redevelopment.

## Development Agreements and Public-Private Partnerships

Development agreements are contracts between the public sector, such as a city or county, or a development authority, and a real estate developer. Often, development agreements specify the development parameters, timing and phasing, and enforcement in exchange for public approval through a land-use planning and permitting process. The development agreement limits development activities to the regulations in effect at the time of agreement, subject to any additional regulatory conditions contained within the development agreement itself.

Development agreements often include specific ways in which the public sector benefits (adapted from Callies and Tappendorf 2014). Some of these benefits may be in the form of monetary or in-kind mitigation. Development agreements should include these elements.[7] Below, I outline provisions of development agreements where both the public and the private sectors commit themselves to providing a public purpose and rely on resources from each other to do so.

## Purposes

Ideally, a development agreement should state its purposes in the context of (1) promoting the local comprehensive plan, development and redevelopment plans, and other planning documents; (2) ensuring the provision of adequate public facilities and services, including the timing and phasing of new or expanded facilities to accommodate the impact of new development; (3) reducing the developer's uncertainty principally by providing regulatory certainty; and (4) assuring certain public benefits relating to the kind of development that occurs.

## Definitions

Development agreements need to define all terms and phrases needed to ensure that all parties understand what they mean and how they may be applied. More definitions may be preferred, rather than fewer, and as a rule of thumb, "when in doubt" define all terms or phrases. At a minimum, definitions should include the following:

- Citations of specific planning and policy documents used to justify the agreement

- Who or what the developer is
- What development means in this context
- That the development agreement means the agreement between specific parties, including its date and other provisions
- That the development permitted includes any building permit, zoning permit, subdivision approval, rezoning, certification, special exception, variance, or any other official action of a local government having the effect of permitting the development of land
- What the governing body is and its authority to regulate land-use development and control[8]
- What the relevant land development regulations are, such as local government zoning, rezoning, subdivision, building construction, or sign regulations or any other regulations controlling the development of land
- A clear definition of what public facilities are, such as capital improvements, including but not limited to transportation, sanitary sewer, solid waste, drainage, potable water, and educational facilities, parks and recreational, and health systems and facilities that have a life expectancy of a certain minimum number of years

## Authority

It is important to cite the sources of authority for the development agreement, including state enablement, local ordinances and resolutions, and other formally adopted policies and procedures, as well as references to provisions of each that give the authority.

## Requirements

Development agreements are contracts between one or more public and private entities. As such, they need to meet requirements provided in authorizing statutes, ordinances, and other public documents. These requirements include procedures, findings, and provisions for implementation.

At a minimum, procedures should include the following:

- One or more public hearings conducted in accordance with statutory, ordinance, or other requirements relating to development agreements
- Notice of the hearing, including the location of the development site, the kind(s) of development activities proposed, and the parameters of development, such as residential units by type, nonresidential space, population and employment densities, building height along with FARs and land-coverage ratios, and where a copy of the proposed development agreement can be acquired (both by address and online)
- The decision, such as approval or rejection, or approval with conditions
- Recordation of the agreement
- Specification of the extent to which the development agreement binds future public officials as well as successors of the developer
- The process for modifying the development agreement

A key element of approval (which may be approval with conditions) is linking the decision to the relevant enabling and ordinance documents and to plans referenced in the Purposes and Definition sections. In particular, there must be findings by the relevant legislative body that

- the development agreement complies with relevant plans;
- the development agreement complies with relevant enabling statutes, local ordinances, and other policies and procedures;
- adequate public facilities and services will be provided;
- public agencies will fulfill specific obligations;
- mitigation of adverse outcomes has been identified and will be met (which may apply to one or more parties to the agreement);
- public benefits have been identified and commitments made to honor them; and
- the term of the development agreement is adequate to fulfill the obligations of all parties.

The development agreement must also include these minimum implementing provisions:

- A legal description of the land subject to the development agreement
- Identification of the property ownership, including legal and equitable ownership conditions
- The term or length of the agreement
- A detailed description of the development to be permitted
- A description of the public facilities needed to accommodate the impacts of the permitted development, noting any current deficiencies of facilities and identifying which party or parties are obligated to improve facilities
- Identification of any part of the development to be reserved for public use, such as easements, parks, plazas, and public spaces inside structures
- Description of the phasing and timing of development
- Schedule of payments or other concessions made by each party to one or more parties
- Other conditions to which the parties have agreed

## Effect

This section of the agreement needs to identify the effect of the development agreement. It should include the following:

- Provision that the agreement governs the approved development during the term of the agreement
- Noted changes in federal law that may affect the development or that may preempt all or part of the agreement
- Stipulation that local government regulations adopted after execution of the development agreement will not be applicable to the approved development unless they are determined through a public hearing process to not be in substantial conflict with the development authorized by the agreement, or the new regulation was anticipated in the agreement, or substantially inaccurate information was provided by the applicant before the agreement was approved

- Other provisions as needed to clarify how the development agreement will be effected

The development agreement should include an enforcement provision allowing any party to enforce its terms against any other party, including their successors, through court action, arbitration, mediation, or another form of dispute resolution.

All three elements—designation of an area that needs public intervention to facilitate redevelopment, a redevelopment plan, and a P3 framework to implement a redevelopment plan through a development agreement—are needed to reduce risk and to maximize public and private benefits.

## Elements of Successful Public-Private Partnerships

The Urban Land Institute sees P3s as the fastest-growing approach to advancing urban economic development and redevelopment. Corrigan et al. (2005) identify ten steps to ensure successful P3 ventures:

- Prepare properly for public-private partnerships.
- Create a shared vision among all of the partners.
- Understand each partner's objectives and the roles of the key players, including staff support, consultants, and advisory groups.
- Be clear about the risks and rewards for partners.
- Establish a clear and rational decision-making process.
- Make sure all partners and key players have done their homework.
- Secure experienced, consistent, and coordinated leadership that is trusted by all partners.
- Communicate early and often with all partners and key players.
- Negotiate a fair deal for all partners.
- Build trust among all partners and key players as a core value.

The Urban Land Institute observes that there may be thousands of successful P3 collaborations. Successful projects have several features in common:

"joint planning, mutual trust, persevering leadership, open communication, and a reasonable sharing of costs, risks, responsibilities, and economic return" (Corrigan et al. 2005, 42).

# Chapter 3

# Real Estate Finance and Development Basics

This chapter creates the foundation for nondevelopers to understand the language and motivation of real estate developers. It starts with a review of key real estate development terms and types (in order of importance within the sections). Because numerous glossaries exist for real estate development and finance, I do not include one in this book. One of the best and most comprehensive, however, is the *Glossary of Commercial Real Estate Terms* provided by the CCIM Institute and the Realtors® Commercial Alliance.[1]

This chapter proceeds with a review of real estate finance concepts, followed by an overview of the real estate development process. It continues with an introduction to the real estate pro forma, including what I believe are the key performance measures facing real estate developers and their public sector partners. It concludes with an orientation to discounted cash flow analysis, including its utility in investment decision making along with its limitations.[2]

## Key Development Terms

*Floor area ratio (FAR)* is the ratio of the total gross floor area on all stories of a structure to the gross area of the building lot; it is primarily used in commercial real estate. A 20,000-square-foot building sitting on a 100,000-square-foot lot would have an FAR of 0.20 regardless of the number of floors it has. The lower the FAR, the more land is used for parking, loading, storage, and other surface activities. Most nonresidential land uses have a FAR of around 0.20, which means that about 80 percent of the land area is used for parking and related surface activities.

*Gross leasable area (GLA)* is the total amount of space in a building.

*Net leasable area (NLA)* is the total square feet of a building less the lobby, elevator, restrooms, and other common spaces.

*Land coverage ratio (LCR)* is the proportion of a building lot that is covered by a structure, expressed in percent or decimal places. A two-story, 20,000-square-foot building with floors of equal size sitting on a 100,000-square-foot parcel of land would have an LCR of 10 percent, or 0.10.

*Parking ratio* is typically the number of parking stalls per 1,000 square feet of gross leasable area. The larger the ratio, the more land area is needed to support parking and the less land area is available for structures. For instance, many suburban communities require seven parking stalls per 1,000 square feet of GLA. Because the typical parking space measures about 19 feet long by 9 feet wide and an equivalent area is needed for maneuvering, about 2,400 square feet of land area is needed for every 1,000 square feet of GLA. Loading and outdoor storage spaces are added to this.

*Residential density* is a measure of the number of dwelling units per unit area of land devoted to residential units, usually expressed in dwelling units per acre. There are several ways to measure residential density:

> **Gross residential density** is the number of dwelling units per unit area of land, including the area needed for streets, easements, and other common areas.
>
> **Net residential density** is the number of dwelling units per unit area of land net of all common areas.

## Key Development Types

Only the most common development types are used in this book. They are included in the financial analysis discussions later in the book as well as in the Excel workbook (http://islandpress.org/ReshapeMetroAmerica). Excluded are hospitals, airports, transit facilities, conference and convention centers, auditoriums and stadiums, religious facilities, group homes such as assisted living and nursing facilities, and incarceration facilities, among others.

## Residential Development

Residential development is broadly categorized into single-family or multifamily distinctions and includes a broad range of development types and densities.

*Single-family detached* refers to a freestanding structure that occupies its own lot. Lot sizes for detached development typically range from under five thousand square feet to one acre or more. Densities for single-family detached development are typically low and range between two to eight dwelling units per acre in suburban areas. A variation that is becoming popular is *cottage units*, which are often less than one thousand square feet in living area and occupy individual, detached lots at twelve or sometimes more units per acre. They are found in highly urbanized areas or resorts.

*Single-family attached* units are two or more dwelling units that share one or more walls with adjacent units and occupy individual lots. They range in density from about twelve units per acre to as many as thirty units per acre. They are often called town houses but sometimes are known as row houses. The higher end of the density range is found in highly urbanized areas, while the lower end is often found in closer-in suburban locations or in planned unit developments comprising different residential options.

*Multifamily residential development* often consists of apartments, which are usually categorized as garden, low-rise, mid-rise, and high-rise structures. In each case, multifamily structures can be rental apartments, condominiums, or cooperatives (where the owner owns a share of the building and not the unit as would be the case with condominiums). Multifamily development is often dictated by market conditions and zoning restrictions.

> **Garden units** are the least expensive to build because they are often concrete slab-on-grade (meaning there are few foundation expenses), typically with wood-frame construction, and have walk-up units on a second (and occasionally a third) floor, thereby avoiding the need for elevators.[3] Typically, floor plans are repeated on each floor. Stairways serve two to four apartments on landings, although some garden apartments are one story. While often designed for lower- and middle-income households, there are also luxury versions of

garden apartments. Surface parking is provided. Among the multifamily types, they have the lowest density at about 12 to 40 units per acre.

**Low-rise units** have similar wood-frame, slab-on-grade construction with repeated floor plans as garden apartments. They are typically three- to five-floor structures with elevators. Parking is provided on the surface or through tuck-under parking garages. Densities range from 40 to 90 units per acre.

**Mid-rise units** are steel-frame or reinforced concrete structures of about four to eight floors in height. Elevators are required, and central halls provide interior unit access. On-site parking structures are usually provided, although in more densely settled areas with transit options, parking may be limited to one vehicle per unit. Densities are from 60 to 120 units per acre.

**High-rise units** are also steel-frame, reinforced concrete structures of nine or more floors with elevators and interior hallways for unit access. Parking is usually underground within the building or in an adjacent parking garage and often requires additional rent.

Residential development distinctions are also made between *owner-occupied* and *renter-occupied* residential units. About a third of the detached and attached residential units are renter occupied, while about a third of the multifamily residential units are owner occupied.

Sometimes development agreements require residential units to be occupied by owners, or only by renters, or occasionally by people based on age (*age-restricted* units), disability (*handicapped/disabled* units), or income (*affordable* units). Except to the extent that these distinctions affect rental revenue, this book does not address these nuances in financial analysis.

### Nonresidential Development

Of the numerous types of nonresidential development, this book focuses on office, retail, lodging, industrial, and structured parking uses.

*Office.* There are several office classes and building types. Office buildings are classified by developers and commercial brokers as A, B, or C.

**Class A** office buildings are usually high-rise buildings in downtowns or major suburban activity centers, are often newer or rehabilitated frequently, and command the highest rent in a region. They are also associated with parking structures on the premises, such as underground or adjacent parking garages.

**Class B** office buildings are lower-rise structures, usually with elevators, or older formerly Class A buildings that have not been rehabilitated. They are often found in downtowns, suburban activity centers, and office parks. They command the next highest rent in the region, in the range of two-thirds the rent for Class A space. While formerly Class A buildings may have on-site structured parking, Class B buildings often rely on surface parking or structured parking shared by other developments, such as public parking garages.

**Class C** office buildings are low-rise structures, often without elevators, and are typically found in suburban activity centers, older office parks, and along commercial corridors. Surface parking is common. Class C buildings command the lowest office rents in the region, perhaps in the range of one-third that of Class A space.

*Retail.* The success of retail development is based heavily on the market demand for the product offered and tenant characteristics. Among the major land uses, retail development may be the most prone to change. During the 1960s and to the 2000s, suburban retail developments were mostly either strip projects along commercial corridors or enclosed shopping malls. The 2000s saw retail development begin to change in important ways. Enclosed malls gave way to open-air designs mimicking small-town main streets, with many rebuilt to include residential and office activities. Big box retail began appearing as infill and redevelopment projects in urban and higher-density suburban areas as multilevel facilities. Coffee shops with small selections of baked and delicatessen goods began appearing seemingly everywhere, often within walking distance of offices, institutions, and higher-density residential areas. Strip commercial centers began being redeveloped as small-scale, mixed-use developments.

One reason why retail development seems to constantly change is that structures housing retail activities usually do not last very long. I have estimated that the typical useful life of a retail structure is twenty years or less, the lowest of all major development types. In contrast, low-rise offices last thirty to fifty years, walk-up multifloor nonretail structures last forty to sixty years, and structures with elevators last fifty to one hundred years and even longer (see Nelson 2004, 2013a).

Moreover, as metropolitan areas expand their transit options, retail will evolve to take advantage of new modes of access. This will be especially the case as bus rapid transit and streetcars/trolleys begin connecting residential with commercial nodes along commercial corridors. While suburban, auto-dependent retail centers will continue to dominate suburban retail activities, the overall share of retail activities along transit corridors and in mixed-use projects large and small will gain increasing share. This will be especially the case at transit-oriented developments (TODs).

Finally, retail may also be among the most vulnerable of all major land uses to small changes in market conditions. As a class, it may be in most need of public-private partnerships to make it financially feasible, especially in targeted infill and redevelopment locations.

Given these trends, I pose the following characterizations of retail developments:[4]

> **Automobile-dependent** developments are the conventional strip centers and malls that dominate the suburban landscape. They include neighborhood, community, regional and super-regional centers, and big boxes and power centers. They will continue to dominate the suburban landscape, but the overall share of retail activities will shift over the next few decades to the new types that move away from the retail mall model and into open-air variations.
>
> **Mixed-use** developments can be large scale (tens to hundreds of acres) or small (under ten acres). They can be part of master-planned greenfield projects for which multimodal access is built into the overall design—and where retail opportunities are distributed broadly across the projects. They can also be part of small-scale infill and redevelopment projects serving the needs of residential and office development in those and nearby areas. Large or small, automobile dependency may dominate, but the projects' configurations allow shorter drives to access retail and also include walking and biking as options.

**Single/limited-use** developments will provide small-scale retail opportunities in neighborhoods focusing on grocery stores, convenience shops, and coffee/baked goods shops within an easy walk of residential units or offices.

**Transit/walkable** activities make up a small share of the total retail space, although that share is growing along fixed-rail transit routes. They are also poised to flourish along low-cost transit routes, such as bus rapid transit and streetcars. These retail activities can include upscale grocery stores housed within high-density residential and office projects, boutique shops, personal services, and a wide range of eating establishments. They are also set within higher-density residential areas where transit is justified. Indeed, my research indicates that there may be sufficient market demand for transit/walkable urbanism that even if all new residential development provided this option of urbanism (see Leinberger 2008) to midcentury, the demand would still not be met (see Nelson 2006, 2013a).

*Lodging.* These activities include low-rise motels, medium to high-rise hotels, long-term residence facilities that can be both apartments and hotel units, and lodging facilities associated with conference and convention centers. They also include resort complexes.

The lodging industry is among the most cyclical of all development types. When the economy declines, occupancy levels can be reduced sharply and stress the financial viability of hotels/motels. On the other hand, when the economy rebounds, the lodging industry may not be able to expand supply to meet demand quickly enough simply because of the delay between deciding to expand lodging facilities and their opening.

Local economic development success may depend on an adequate supply of lodging options. For one thing, lodging facilities are critical to attracting visitors, conferences, and conventions that bring new cash to the local economy. For another, they can stimulate the redevelopment of an area through the collateral activities these visitors may engage in, such as shopping, dining, and cultural activities.

*Industrial.* Industrial activities mean much more than manufacturing. Generally, these activities refer to land-extensive activities that have fewer workers per one thousand square feet of GLA than do office, retail, medical, or other activities and require substantially more land area for loading/unloading trucks. Activities can include manufacturing, assembly, warehousing, storage, and distribution. Industrial activities usually occupy three kinds of structures:

> **Manufacturing** structures for the processing of raw materials and the assembly of components into final products. These activities usually require accessibility to major highways, rail services, and airports. The structures have very low employee-to-area ratios, thus reducing their need for parking, but they also have substantial demand for truck accessibility. Structures range from a few hundred thousand to a few million square feet in GLA.
>
> **Warehouse/distribution** structures for bulk storage/warehousing, refrigerated distribution, and rack-supported distribution. Like manufacturing, these structures have very low employee-to-area ratios, thus reducing their need for parking, but they also have substantial demand for truck accessibility. Structures also range from a few hundred thousand to a few million square feet in GLA.
>
> **Flex** industrial sites, which are diverse and often include a hybrid mix of office and warehousing uses, with occasional assembly. Flex structures tend to consist of one- or two-story buildings ranging from twenty thousand to one hundred thousand square feet and usually combine office with warehousing activities. Among the industrial activities, they have the highest employee-to-area ratio and need both parking for workers and visitors and a truck loading/unloading area.

## Mixed-Use Development

Mixed-use developments integrate an array of different land uses, and their size can vary from a single building to millions of square feet. Often, a resilient development includes a healthy combination of retail, office, and residential units, and recently developments have also added other uses, such as recreation and hotels. A successful mixed-use development incorporates great pedestrian design, provides a vibrant mix of uses within a space, and, most importantly, both serves the public vision and satisfies the private parties involved.

It is essential to understand that the greater the mix of uses a development has, the greater the financial risk is for the parties involved. Thorough market research and collaboration between the public and private parties involved is a key for a mixed-use development not only to be successful financially but also to provide the community with a vibrant locality.

The larger the size of a development, the more complex the issue of parking becomes. Often, mixed-use projects have parking in multilevel structures due to lack of space. The price of parking structures can make a project undesirable, especially if the structure must be built underground. To deal with parking, the developer and the municipality must collaborate on parking policy and understand shared parking options and parking ratios of different uses to best maximize parking efficiencies (Willson 2013b). Thankfully, with increasing transit options and growing bicycle use, communities across the nation are reevaluating their parking policies.

## *Parking*

Even in the most transit/walking/biking-rich urbanized areas, parking is needed to round out land-use accessibility. Of course, the less rich an urbanized area is in options other than the automobile, the more parking is needed.

Parking structures come in many forms and purposes. The most common is the *surface lot*. An acre of surface parking can accommodate about one hundred parking stalls. The next most common structure is the *aboveground parking garage* followed by the *underground parking garage* version. In between surface and garage options is *tuck-under parking*, where surface parking stalls are tucked under structures much like single-family garages are tucked under the second floors of homes. A new version of parking is emerging called *mechanical parking*, in which robotic devices are used to lift and retrieve cars from elevated storage slots. I devote a section to financing parking structures in chapter 4.

## Real Estate Finance Concepts

Real estate investments are risky. Real estate investors not only risk losing their money but also risk not making as much as they could with a better investment of time and money. Investors assess real estate opportunities principally from a rate-of-return perspective given risks and considering return from other, safer investment options. Key real estate investment concepts are summarized here.

### Return on Investment

The most generic rate-of-return calculation is called return on investment (ROI):

> Return on investment = (Gain from investment – Cost of investment) / (Cost of investment)

To run the formula, however, one needs to know what the "investment" is. Following are examples of total project cost, equity, and capital investments.

### Unleveraged Return on Investment

The most basic bottom-line measure of real estate investment performance is called the "unleveraged return on investment" because it is based on the total project cost, not just what equity investors contribute. It can be calculated for any given year and across multiple years. For a single year, suppose an investor builds a home for a total cost of $450,000 and then sells it for $500,000 net of sales expenses. The unleveraged ROI is as follows:

> *Unleveraged ROI*
> Price = $500,000
> Cost = $450,000
> Gain = $50,000
> ROI, unleveraged = 10%

## Return on Investment Equity (or "Leveraged Return")

A variation of return on investment is measuring return on equity, which is the amount of money an investor puts into the project after all other sources of financing —such as banks—are accounted for. Investors use their money, called equity, to "leverage" other money. Suppose the home builder borrowed $300,000 to build a home that cost $450,000. The equity would be $150,000. Suppose the home sells for $500,000. The leveraged return on equity would be as follows:

*Leveraged ROI*
    Price = $500,000
    Cost = $450,000
    Loan = $300,000
    Equity = $150,000
    Gain = $50,000
    ROI, leveraged = 33%

Notice that in this example the leveraged ROI is several times larger than the unleveraged ROI. The reason is that the equity leverages loans to build the project. Investors often worry more about return on equity because it is their own money, but they also have more to lose. In this example, the home could sell for $300,000 or $200,000 less than the target sales price, and the equity investor would lose all of the money invested.

I will next present the basic concepts of real estate finance relating to income-producing property. These concepts underlie most long-term real estate investments that generate income from rents, leases, and other sources. Key concepts include net operating income, capitalization rate and market value, debt service, before-tax cash flow, and the return on cash or equity dividend rate, also known as cash-on-cash.

## Net Operating Income

The net operating income (NOI) of a project is total income less total costs excluding debt service. It is calculated as follows:[5]

Gross Scheduled Income (GSI)

+ Miscellaneous income (MI), such as from coin machines

= Potential gross income (PGI)

− Vacancy and bad debt (VBD)

= Effective gross income (EGI)

− Operating expenses (OE)

= Net operating income (NOI)

Suppose an apartment building has one hundred rental units averaging $1,000 per month in rent. The vacant rate might be four percent, and renters who do not pay rent reduce rental income by another one percent. The coin machines in the apartment building might generate $30,000 annually. Operating costs—including building management, insurance, taxes, cleaning, general maintenance, and routine repairs—might run $3,000 per unit. The NOI is calculated as shown in table 3.1.

**Table 3.1.**
Calculating Net Operating Income (NOI)

| Figure | Description |
| --- | --- |
| $1,200,000 | GSI at $1,000/unit per month |
| $30,000 | MI |
| $1,230,000 | PGI |
| 5.00% | VBD rate (applied to GSI) |
| $60,000 | VBD amount |
| $1,170,000 | EGI |
| $300,000 | OE at $3,000/unit per year |
| $870,000 | NOI |

There are variations in nomenclature as well as detail (operating expenses can be broken into dozens of subcategories for instance), but these are the general calculation steps leading to the NOI. However, missing from these calculation steps is a concept called "replacement reserve" (RR). This is an amount of money set aside each year so that when large capital expenses are incurred, such as a new roof, the money is available for this purpose. This would reduce the NOI. But if the RR funds are not spent before the building is sold, they are retained by the seller anyway. The buyer will have done due diligence, which includes identifying needed repairs and upgrades, so the purchase price will reflect these adjustments. Finally, because the typical RR allocation is often small (or nonexistent), I exclude it for simplicity of analysis. Nonetheless, RR can be included in the operating expenses step at the analyst's option.

### Capitalization Rate and Market Value

The NOI is used to estimate the market value (V) of a real estate investment using this formula:

$$V = NOI/R$$

where R is the capitalization rate, which is also called the cap rate. The cap rate is the ratio between the NOI and its market value. It is often based on the recent sales prices (P) of comparable properties. Suppose five projects comparable to the example were sold in the past month for an average of $15 million, and each averaged $900,000 annually in NOI. (This information is usually obtained by commercial brokers or real estate consultants.) The capitalization rate for these properties is

$$R = P/NOI = \$900,000/\$15,000,000 = 0.06 = 6.00\%$$

The example apartment project would have a market value of

$$V = NOI/R = \$870,000/6.00\% = \$14,500,000$$

### Debt Service

Most real estate investors borrow money to build or otherwise purchase property. As I will show later in this chapter, there are many forms of loans. The most common is a primary loan from a bank or an institutional lender, such as an insurance company or a pension fund. These lenders typically offer between 60 percent and 80 percent of the value of a project. Mezzanine financing (so called because it is the middle between a primary lender and the equity investor) often provides the difference between the primary lender and the equity investor, which is normally 5 to 20 percent of the project cost or purchase price. In the apartment building example, assume the value is $14,500,000, a primary lender offers 65 percent financing at 5 percent over thirty years, and a mezzanine lender will offer 15 percent financing at 10 percent over thirty years (both loans would be due in five years unless renegotiated). The equity investor puts up the remaining 20 percent. In this example, the debt service schedule for the primary and mezzanine lenders is (1) $607,145 of primary loan debt service; (2) $229,046 of mezzanine loan debt service; and (3) $836,191 of total annual debt service.

I offer more detailed comments about real estate capital below.

### Before-Tax Cash Flow

The amount of money left to distribute to the equity investors is the net operating income less debt service. This is called before-tax cash flow (BTCF):

$$BTCF = NOI - DS = \$870,000 - \$836,191 = \$33,809$$

The equity investors would pay a tax on this, so the final calculation would be called after-tax cash flow (ATCF). However, this book does not delve into tax issues because they include reducing BTCF by depreciation, which varies by property type and even by components within the property (e.g., roofs have a different depreciation rate than carpets), different tax rates for different kinds of income (ordinary income such as wages and capital gains), different tax rates for different kinds of investors (such as corporations and individuals), different tax rates for different levels of income (top income people pay a 39.5 percent tax rate but many investors pay less, plus Social Security and Medicaid tax rates will vary), and tax structures that vary by state and even by some cities. While ATCF calculations are crucial for real estate investors, they are mostly immaterial for planners, economic development professionals, public officials, and the general public. What matters to these groups is whether publicly provided resources achieve reasonable rates of return based on before-tax expectations.

## Return on Cash/Equity Dividend Rate (Also Known as Cash-on-Cash)

While the nature of real estate investment is to see equity investment gain over time—typically ten or more years—many also want to earn money on their investment in the short term. They wish to receive a "dividend" on their equity, which is known as the equity dividend rate or, more commonly, cash-on-cash. Since the Great Recession, a common minimum cash-on-cash target has been ten percent. It is calculated as follows:

*Cash-on-Cash*
 BTFC = $33,809
 Equity = $240,000
 Equity dividend rate = 14.1%

# The Real Estate Development Process

The real estate development process is unpredictable, complex, and seemingly never the same. James A. Graaskamp (1981, 1) observed:

> *Unlike many mass-production industries, each real estate project is unique and the development process is so much a creature of the political process that society has a new opportunity with each major project to negotiate, debate, and reconsider the basic issues of an enterprise economy, i.e., who pays, who benefits, who risks, and who has standing to participate in the decision process. Thus the development process remains a high-silhouette topic for an articulate and politically sophisticated society.*

Graaskamp (1981, 1) also speculated on when the real estate development industry was formed:

> *Someone rolled a rock to the entrance of a cave and created an enclosed space for his family—a warmer, more defensible shelter, distinct from the surrounding environment. This can be called the first real estate de-*

*velopment. Since then real estate activity has evolved and taken many forms to meet the needs of man and his society. Once based on need and custom, real estate is now based on social economics and statute.*

Graaskamp (1981, 1) went on to observe:

*The creation and management of space-time on earth is termed real estate development. Real estate developments range from a simple cave to complex technology of the Park Avenue skyscraper. Like a manufactured product, a real estate project is part of a larger physical system programmed to achieve long-term objectives, but each real estate project is also a small business enterprise of its own. Thus, the development process is a continuum of construction technology, financing, marketing skills, administrative controls, and rehabilitation required to operate the real estate enterprise over many years.*

**Table 3.2.**
Pro Forma Apartment Building Analysis under Current Zoning

| Construction Cost | | |
|---|---|---|
| *Item* | *Amount* | *Label/Description* |
| Land area | 1.00 | Acres |
| Zoning density allowed | 25 | Units per acre |
| Units | 25 | Units |
| Parking spaces per unit | 2.00 | |
| Parking spaces | 50 | |
| Average unit size | 900 | |
| Project size | 22,500 | Square feet |
| Floor area ratio | 0.52 | FAR |
| **Hard costs** | | |
| Cost per surface parking stall | $5,000 | |
| Parking cost | $250,000 | |
| Construction cost | $145 | Per square foot |
| Construction cost | $130,500 | Per unit |
| Construction cost project | $3,262,500 | |
| Total project hard costs | $3,512,500 | |

**Soft costs**

| | |
|---|---|
| Architecture/engineering | $100,000 |
| Permit fees | $200,000 |
| Construction loan fees | $200,000 |
| Overhead, marketing | $100,000 |
| Total project soft costs | $600,000 |
| **Land costs** | **$1,500,000** |
| **Total project costs** | **$5,612,500** |

**Revenue Analysis**

| Item | Amount | Label/Description |
|---|---|---|
| Average monthly rent | $1,250 | R |
| Gross scheduled income, monthly | $31,250 | GSI |
| Miscellaneous income rate | 2.00% | |
| Miscellaneous income amount, monthly | $625 | MI |
| Potential gross income, monthly | $31,875 | PGI |
| Potential gross income, project, annual | $382,500 | |
| Vacancy/bad debt rate | 5.00% | |
| Vacancy/bad debt amount | $19,125 | VBD |
| Effective gross income | $363,375 | EGI |
| Annual operating expenses per unit | $3,200 | OE |
| Annual operating expenses, project | $80,000 | |
| Net operating income | $283,375 | NOI |
| Capitalization rate | 0.06 | |
| Capitalized value | $4,722,917 | |

**Summary Analysis**

| Item | Amount |
|---|---|
| Capitalized value | $4,722,917 |
| Total project costs | $5,612,500 |
| Net project return | ($889,583) |

The fluidity of the real estate development process notwithstanding, leading texts offer their own view of it. *Real Estate Development: Principles and Process* (fourth edition; Miles et al. 2007) devotes much of the book to detailing critical stages of the real estate development process:

- Stage 1: Inception of an idea
- Stage 2: Refinement of the idea
- Stage 3: Feasibility
- Stage 4: Contract negotiation
- Stage 5: Formal commitment
- Stage 6: Construction
- Stage 7: Completion and formal opening
- Stage 8: Property, assets, and portfolio management

Daniel B. Kohlhepp's (2012) review of all of the leading real estate texts found little consistency among them, however. Instead, he creates a matrix composed of seven stages, each with eight activities. His seven stages are especially relevant to this book. In summary, with permission, I have paraphrased Professor Kohlhepp's insights here:

- Stage 1: Land-Banking, in which public or private sectors act by design, such as purchasing property in the path of development, or by accident, such as acquiring land anticipating to build something but then not, or using the land for open storage or another nondeveloped purpose.
- Stage 2: Land Packaging and Entitlement, in which the "Land Packager" acquires land from the land bank, adds value to it by securing planning and land-use control decisions, which are called entitlements, and sells it to the land developer.
- Stage 3: Land Development, in which a developer acquires the land with all its entitlements, installs the necessary infrastructure, and sells the parcel or individual lots carved out of it to a builder.
- Stage 4: Building Development, in which a builder acquires the finished land from the land developer and proceeds to build products such as homes, multifamily units, retail outlets, offices, or other uses.
- Stage 5: Operating, which is usually limited to rental property where a "Building Operator" leases up and manages the property. Often, these are institutional investors, such as insurance companies, pension funds, and real estate investment trusts (REITs).
- Stage 6: Renovation, in which the property has aged toward (or beyond) its economic useful life and is sold to a "Property Renovator"

who repurposes it. Examples include historic preservation, converting warehouses into lofts, converting former Class A office towers into apartments or condominiums, and so forth.

• Stage 7: Redevelopment, in which, ultimately, an owner (perhaps a new one) decides to tear down the old and rebuild—thus starting the real estate development cycle over. This book focuses on this stage of the real estate development process.

## The Real Estate Pro Forma

The key tool to evaluate whether a particular real estate development is worthwhile is the "pro forma." This is an estimate of the acquisition costs (including construction costs, if relevant), revenues, expenses, and net income. It can be either for a single year or for several years (such as with discounted cash flow analysis, which will be presented later). While the general structure of the pro forma is routine, its application to different kinds of real estate developments can vary. For details across all the major development types, I recommend Richard B. Peiser's and David Hamilton's (2012) text *Professional Real Estate Development: The ULI Guide to the Business.*

A pro forma is usually composed of these elements:

Project characteristics
Project costs
Project revenues
Net operating income
Capitalization rate and market value
Net project return

I will illustrate these concepts and how they make up the pro forma in the case of a one-acre parcel of land to be developed as apartments. In this example, I will show a pro forma based on current zoning conditions (table 3.2) indicating the project to be financially infeasible. I will then show the pro forma if zoning is changed to allow a financially feasible apartment project to be built on the site.

## Project Characteristics

Project characteristics usually include specifics about the site and its development, such as land area and size of the structure in square feet and/or rental units (such as apartment units). Suppose that under current zoning, the allowable density is twenty-five units per acre and two parking stalls per unit. As will be seen, a project conforming to current zoning may not be feasible. This is shown in table 3.2. Perhaps the local community changes the zoning for this and other nearby parcels to allow for fifty units per acre and just one parking stall per unit. Table 3.3 reflects these new project characteristics and goes on to show the project may be financially feasible.

**Table 3.3.**
Pro Forma Apartment Building Analysis after Zone Change

| Construction Cost | | |
|---|---|---|
| *Item* | *Amount* | *Label/Description* |
| Land area | 1.00 | Acres |
| Zoning density allowed | 50 | Units per acre |
| Units | 50 | Units |
| Parking spaces per unit | 1.00 | |
| Parking spaces | 50 | |
| Average unit size | 900 | |
| Project size | 45,000 | Square feet |
| Floor area ratio | 1.03 | FAR |
| **Hard costs** | | |
| Cost per surface parking stall | $5,000 | |
| Parking cost | $250,000 | |
| Construction cost | $145 | Per square foot |
| Construction cost | $130,500 | Per unit |
| Construction cost, project | $6,525,000 | |
| Total project hard costs | $6,775,000 | |
| **Soft costs** | | |
| Architecture/engineering | $150,000 | |
| Permit fees | $400,000 | |
| Construction loan fees | $400,000 | |
| Overhead, marketing | $150,000 | |

**Soft costs**

| | |
|---|---|
| Total project soft costs | $1,100,000 |
| **Land costs** | **$1,500,000** |
| **Total project costs** | **$9,375,000** |

**Revenue Analysis**

| Item | Amount | Label/Description |
|---|---|---|
| Average monthly rent | $1,250 | R |
| Gross scheduled income, monthly | $62,500 | GSI |
| Miscellaneous income rate | 2.00% | |
| Miscellaneous income amount, monthly | $1,250 | MI |
| Potential gross income, monthly | $63,750 | PGI |
| Potential gross income, project | $765,000 | |
| Vacancy/bad debt rate | 5.00% | |
| Vacancy/bad debt amount | $38,250 | VBD |
| Effective gross income | $726,750 | EGI |
| Annual operating expenses per unit | $3,200 | OE |
| Annual operating expenses, project | $160,000 | |
| Net operating income | $566,750 | NOI |
| Capitalization rate | 0.06 | |
| Capitalized value | $9,445,833 | |

**Summary Analysis**

| Item | Amount |
|---|---|
| Capitalized value | $9,445,833 |
| Total project costs | $9,375,000 |
| Net project return | $70,833 |

## Project Cost

There are three basic parts to project costs: hard costs, soft costs, and land costs. Hard costs relate to "bricks-and-mortar" expenditures for constructing the building and related amenities such as parking. If off-site improvements are needed, such as access lanes and street lights, they would be included here. Soft costs relate to planning, design, legal, permitting processes and fees, construction financing, and other costs not related to hard costs or the land. Land costs include all costs associated with acquiring land, including title, legal, and closing costs and any real estate transfer taxes and fees, environmental assessments, and commissions paid by the developer.

## Net Operating Income

Recall from earlier in this chapter that NOI is revenues actually received less operating expenses. The net operating income of a project is total income less total costs excluding debt service.

## Capitalization Rate and Market Value

The next step in the pro forma process is to estimate the market value of a project using the capitalization as reviewed earlier.

The higher the cap rate, the lower the building value and vice versa. This is illustrated in table 3.4, which reports a sample of capitalization rates for 2012 and converts them to property values assuming $1 million in NOI. Notice that the lowest cap rates and therefore the highest values were of high- and moderate-income apartment investments. Also, downtown offices had considerably more favorable cap rates than suburban offices.

Cap rates vary with economic cycles, the cost of money, market demand, and perceptions of long-term market stability. Generally, cap rates for properties closer to downtowns are lower, meaning values are higher, than farther away. Cap rates for rental residential property tend to be among the lowest of commercial rental properties and thus have higher values for the same NOI than office, retail, and lodging properties.

## Net Project Return

The calculation using the static pro forma approach is to compare the capitalized market value of the project to development costs. If the figure is negative, as it is in table 3.2, the project is projected to have a negative return over a typical holding period (usually five to twenty years). Such is

**Table 3.4.**
Sample Capitalization Rates, 2012

| Sector | Cap Rate 2012 | Value at $1 Million NOI |
|---|---|---|
| Apartment: high income | 5.67 | $17.6M |
| Apartment: moderate income | 6.11 | $16.4M |
| Central city office | 6.15 | $16.3M |
| Regional malls | 6.37 | $15.7M |
| Warehouse industrial | 6.92 | $14.5M |
| Neighborhood/community shopping centers | 6.97 | $14.3M |
| Full-service hotels | 7.27 | $13.8M |
| Power centers | 7.42 | $13.5M |
| R&D industrial | 7.62 | $13.1M |
| Suburban office | 7.90 | $12.7M |
| Limited-service hotels | 8.16 | $12.3M |

Source: Adapted from Urban Land Institute (2012, 48).

the case with this example project at the current allowable density, so investing in it is not recommended. On the other hand, the local community may realize that the current zoning is antiquated or not conducive to real estate investment. As shown in the Long Beach case study in chapter 1, the community may decide to update zoning to facilitate new development. Suppose zoning is changed to allow twice the number of residential units and half the number of parking stalls than with the current zoning. The project would appear to become financially feasible (though just barely), and real estate development may occur.

Static pro forma analysis does not truly consider the time dimension of real estate investment. This is overcome through "discounted cash flow" analysis, which is explained later in this chapter.

# The Capital Stack

Real estate investment requires capital, or money, and usually lots of it. The typical real estate deal requires multiple sources of capital in blocks, usually referred to as tranches, composing a "capital stack" (as illustrated in fig. 3.1).[6] The capital stack is the total amount of capital made available for a real estate development

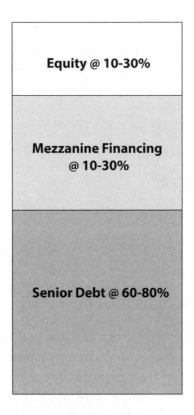

**Figure 3.1.** Illustrative capital stack for financing real estate development. Senior debt is commonly used to finance the largest loan-to-value (L/V) share of a real estate development, and it is first in line to receive revenues. Mezzanine financing fills the gap between senior debt and the equity put up by investors; it is also second in line for revenues. Typically, equity financing is the smallest share but is also last in line to receive revenues. (In the public domain; created by Arthur C. Nelson and redrawn by Allison Spain)

and usually consists of debt, hybrid forms of debt and equity, and equity. Each layer of the stack needs higher rates of return to justify its risk of not earning the target rate of return or even of losing its entire position. Conversely, lower levels of the stack carry less risk and so returns are lower.

In its simplest form, the capital stack comprises "senior" debt, in which a bank or institutional lender provides the largest share of financing at the lowest rate, and has the most secure position in the real estate investment—it has the "first call" on revenue. Mezzanine (or secondary) financing makes up the difference between the senior debt and the equity investors—hence they are in the middle and have "second call" on revenue. Finally, there is "equity" financing, for which the real estate investors put their own capital into the project; they have the most to lose since they are last in line to receive revenue. Debt, whether it is called a loan or a mortgage, is usually in the form of a promissory note secured by a deed of trust that serves as collateral and is recorded against the property. If the real estate property fails to pay its debt service, the holder of the note can foreclose the property to collect on the promissory note. But the collateral for senior debt is often just the property itself; the investors are not personally responsible for paying off the debt (unless they commit fraud or in other ways violate certain terms of the deed of trust). Because the most senior debt is paid first, its risk is lowest and thus its rate of return is often the lowest. At the other end of the continuum, equity capital is last in line and thus needs a higher rate of return to justify the risk. In the simple capital stack, we see senior debt, mezzanine financing, and equity.

> **Senior debt:** The senior or "first position" lender is the safest position in the capital stack because it has the first option on capital upon sale or transfer of the property, bankruptcy, or foreclosure. While the loan-to-value (L/V) ratios vary based on product type (with retail often being the most risky and rental apartments being the least) and geographic location (with suburban fringe often being the most risky and city center being the least), a real estate development is typically financed with an L/V ratio of 60 percent to 80 percent of the project value (based on appraisals) once completed. Because of its low risk, it typically earns the lowest rate of return on capital, ranging about 250 to 400 basis points (2.50 to 4.00 interest points) above the prime lending rate. (If the prime lending rate is 4.00 percent, the senior debt will typically range from 6.50 percent to 8.00 percent.) The term of the senior debt can range from about five years to twenty or more years. If institutional investors are involved, such as pension funds and insurance companies, the term usually runs several decades, though the interest charged may be reset periodically to reflect then-existing borrowing conditions. In complex projects, there can be many sources of senior debt. The cost of capital for lower positions is slightly higher than for the first position.

**Mezzanine financing**: The next segment of the capital stack is what is often called mezzanine financing because it sits between the senior debt and the equity the investors need. (It is also known as junior, secondary, and bridge financing.) Mezzanine debt is less secure than senior debt but more secure than investor equity. The security for a mezzanine loan is often not the property itself but an ownership interest. Therefore, this kind of financing is sometimes called hybrid financing because it includes both debt that must be repaid and equity since the property itself is often not the collateral. Mezzanine debt is usually short term—less than five years and typically one to three years—and, given its higher risk, costs 200 to 300 basis points (2.00 to 3.00 percentage points) more than the senior debt; the rate of return can vary widely, however. When used, the combination of senior and mezzanine debt can cover up to 90 percent or sometimes more of the total project cost. In large real estate projects, there can be several sources of mezzanine financing, each with their own terms.

**Equity:** The last and usually smallest segment of the capital stack is equity financing. Equity is the difference between total project costs and all other debt available to cover those costs. Equity investors are last in line to receive payments and as such typically require the highest return on capital. Equity investors also hold unsecured positions in the property, so there is collateral to protect their interests, as there is for debt investors.

Because they carry the highest level of risk, equity investors usually expect higher returns. This comes in two forms: (1) cash-on-cash, which is calculated as the percent received by the equity investors from project cash flow in relation to equity contributions made; and (2) total project returns after sale calculated as the present value of net sales price plus annual cash-on-cash. This is the "discounted cash flow" analysis that I will introduce in the next section. Under market conditions in the 2010s, equity investors expect annual cash-on-cash returns ranging from about 5 percent (for the least risky investments, such as an apartment building closer in) to about 10 percent or more (for the riskiest investments, such as strip malls in suburban fringe locations). Total project returns needed to justify the equity investment range from about 20 percent to 30 percent.

## Discounted Cash Flow Analysis

Discounted cash flow (DCF) analysis accounts for the stream of revenues and expenses over time, discounting them to the present. It is a common way to evaluate the present value of a real estate investment held over time. In this way, different real estate investment opportunities can be fairly compared, resulting in more informed decision making by investors. Unlike the static pro forma analysis, which is geared to give a general impression of project value when a project is mature, DCF analysis allows investors to measure their rate of return.

The DCF has emerged as the principal tool to guide long-term investment decision making, especially for real estate. It is surprising to learn that DCF has been a mainstay in real estate curricula only since the 1960s. A principal advantage of DCF is that it provides a common way to compare completely different investment alternatives. DCF can also be used to compare alternative assumptions.

DCF has its limitations, such as a tendency to overly discount investments that otherwise are in good locations and offer more future options than standard real estate products. Indeed, Christopher B. Leinberger puts most of the blame for the Great Recession on America's overproduction of up to nineteen building types that have no lasting value or alternative uses.[7] He advocates a role for "patient equity" in which a partner provides financial and other resources at the early stage of the project but waits (i.e., is patient) to receive revenues until the project matures. I discuss how this works conceptually in chapter 4.

DCF analysis works best when future cash flows are certain, such as in comparing the present value of different real estate investment opportunities, each with long-term lease contracts and reasonably well known costs. In the absence of firm long-term commitments, assumptions are needed to run DCF models. While costs can be reasonably well known, assumptions are needed on future borrowing rates, vacancies, and, especially, target rates of return. Moreover, what may be in fashion today may be out of fashion by the end of the investment analysis horizon. For instance, enclosed malls are losing favor to open, higher-intensity mixed-use mall projects. In addition, assumptions need to account for competition—for example, perhaps the market can support two 50,000-square-foot strip centers along a given commercial corridor, so DCF modeling can compare returns from both, but what if four strip centers are ultimately built during the same investment analysis period?

Moreover, what if the long-term discount rate should be far lower than assumed (and thus present values should be higher) if the future market favors closer-in redevelopment locations over locations farther out? For instance, in 2000, no one predicted $4 per gallon gasoline by 2008 or even 2014. Suburban investment rates of return assumptions considered known knowns, such as rental and vacancy rates, and may have been able to hedge on known unknowns, such as the future competition in the same market or even some increase in gasoline prices, but assumptions were unlikely to consider unknown unknowns, such as overbuilding suburban residential housing stock, leading to the Great Recession, the effects of which would linger for a decade or more afterward.[8] In retrospect, investors in strip centers in suburban commercial corridors may have incurred substantial opportunity costs by overinvesting in those locations and underinvesting elsewhere.

Like Christopher Leinberger (2001, 2007), my view is that DCF tends to distort long-term investment decision making favoring investment in types for which there is a historic track record—such as suburban commercial corridor strip centers serving baby boomers at the peak of their housing needs from the middle 1980s to the late 2000s—and disfavoring walkable infill and redevelopment locations meeting the needs of the emerging demography by overly discounting investments that anticipate market repositioning. Nonetheless, DCF is the most widely accepted method of evaluating the long-term return from real estate investments.

The workbook accompanying this book includes a set of Excel worksheets, all of which have DCF programmed into them, but I do not present the mathematical details of DCF analysis here. Standard real estate textbooks review the mathematical mechanics of the procured, and James R. DeLisle has an excellent online tutorial.[9]

## Debt-Coverage Ratio

Lenders need to be assured that sufficient revenue is being generated by the project to cover debt service and then some. The debt-coverage ratio (DCR) is used to analyze this. The DCR is calculated as follows:

DCR = Effective gross income/Debt service ⟩ 1.25

where a ratio of 1.25 is often desired because effective gross income is then 25 percent more than debt service. Because many projects take a year or more to lease up, the DCR is often based on the third year of operations, called the year of stabilization, though this can vary.

## Performance Benchmarks

Because investors' equity is the most vulnerable to loss, they want the highest reasonable rate of return to justify that risk. Consider the options available to investors. Federally backed securities earn 3 percent to 5 percent annually. Tax-free bonds generate the equivalent of about a 6 percent return before taxes. Triple A–rated corporate debt earns about 6 percent annually. The stock market averages about 8 percent annually in normal years. Being a mezzanine financier would bring 10 percent to 14 percent annually. Considering other opportunities relative to risk, an equity investor who is last in line will need the highest rate of return to justify the investment. Investors rely on three key rate-of-return performance measures in comparing investment opportunities:

Equity dividend rate (commonly referred to as cash-on-cash)
Project rate of return (before-tax unleveraged return)
Equity rate of return (before-tax leveraged return)

*Equity dividend rate (cash-on-cash).* The equity dividend rate (EDR) is more commonly called the cash-on-cash return. When a project is built or purchased, much of the price can be covered by one or more loans. Loan-to-value (L/V) ratios of 60 to 75 percent are common for nonresidential projects, such as office buildings, apartments, and shopping centers, but this means investors have to cover the rest. This is their "equity" in a project. In addition to any capital gains when the project sells after several years, investors want an annual return on their equity. This return is the EDR or cash-on-cash, and it is calculated as follows:

EDR = (Before-tax cash flow/Equity)

EDR targets vary widely depending on investor objectives, tax situation, expectations of long-term appreciation, type of property, and so forth. Generally, EDR targets range from about 6 percent to 10 percent, though lower and higher targets are common depending on the characteristics of the property and of the investor. For instance, a redevelopment authority or other nonprofit group may be an investor, and if it is exempt from federal and state income taxes, it could justify a 5.5 percent EDR, as it is equivalent to a before-tax EDR of about 10 percent. Moreover, if that group's principal motivation is to stimulate collateral development in the area, it might settle for an even lower EDR.

*Project rate of return (before-tax unleveraged investment)* and *equity rate of return (before-tax leveraged investment)*. In addition to cash-on-cash, real estate investors commonly make investment decisions based on long-term expectations of return. What they are after is an average annual rate of return (before taxes) that combines annual net revenues and long-term capital gains into a blended estimate that is sufficient to reward their risk (and personal anxiety). These long-term returns are based on either the overall cost of the whole project (unleveraged investment) or just on their equity (leveraged investment).

There are two measures of long-term rate of return: internal rate of return (IRR) and net present value (NPV). Most real estate investors use the IRR to guide their decision-making process. Conceptually, the IRR is the average annual rate of return considering annual net cash flow and net sales proceeds (the project sales process less outstanding loans and sales expenses) when the project is sold, in relation to either the total project cost (unleveraged investment) or the equity (leveraged investment). It is always reported as a percentage. If the projected unleveraged return is 10 percent even though the investors want 12 percent, obviously the target is not met and investors may look elsewhere.

The NPV approach is another way to estimate average annual returns using the same cost and revenue data, but it is reported in dollars. Its advantage over the IRR calculation is that investors can see the difference between the target and projected rate of return in dollars. If the projected unleveraged return is zero dollars, it means that the 12 percent target is achieved, but if the projected return is negative $1 million, it means the project falls $1 million short in achieving the target. This amount is helpful to public sector partners because they know the actual dollar amount a project's projected return falls short and thus whether more leveraging assistance may be needed. On the other hand, if the NPV is plus $1 million, those same public sector partners might consider a smaller leveraging assistance package.

I recommend using both the IRR and the NPV because they inform both private and public sector partners in terms each understands best.

The project rate of return is based on the acquisition price of the project, whether new or purchased turnkey. The riskier the project is, the higher the rate of return that is needed. As a rule of thumb, the target project rate of return is about twice the commercial lending rate plus or minus about a quarter depending on specific project characteristics. Thus, if the commercial lending rate is 6 percent, as during the first half of the 2010s (based on a thirty-year mortgage period), the project rate of return would be 12 percent, ranging perhaps between 9 percent and 15 percent.

The equity rate of return is based on the equity contributed by the investors, which is why it is also called the leveraged return. As a rule of thumb, the target equity rate of return is about twice the target unleveraged return plus or minus about a quarter. If the unleveraged target is 12 percent, the leveraged target may be 25 percent, ranging between 20 percent and 30 percent depending on specific project and investor factors.

Private investors often calculate both project and equity rate of return after taxes. The reason is that cash flow during the holding period is subject to ordinary income taxation (with losses either carried forward to future years or applied to positive income in a real estate investment portfolio) and profit or loss from sale is subject to long-term capital gains tax treatment. The tax consequences to investors are difficult for public sector analysts to know. For

**Table 3.5.**
Project Annual Cash Flow Summary

| Item | Rate | Escalation | Year 1 | Year 3 | Year 5 | Year 10 |
|---|---|---|---|---|---|---|
| GSI | | 3.00% | $750,000 | $795,675 | $844,132 | $978,580 |
| Miscellaneous income | | | $15,000 | $15,914 | $16,883 | $19,572 |
| PGI | | | $765,000 | $811,589 | $861,014 | $998,151 |
| Less: Vacancy | 4.00% | | $30,600 | $32,464 | $34,441 | $39,926 |
| Less: Other | 1.00% | | $7,650 | $8,116 | $8,610 | $9,982 |
| EGI | | | $726,750 | $771,009 | $817,964 | $948,244 |
| Less: OE | | 3.00% | $160,000 | $169,744 | $180,081 | $208,764 |
| NOI | | | $566,750 | $601,265 | $637,882 | $739,480 |
| Less: Debt service | | | $472,146 | $472,146 | $472,146 | $472,146 |
| Net cash flow | | | $94,604 | $129,119 | 165,736 | $267,334 |
| Cash-on-Cash | | | 3.36% | 4.49% | 5.89% | 9.51% |

*Note:* Intervening years have been excluded for brevity.

one thing, different investors have different income tax brackets and even different entities that are created for their own tax purposes. For another, investors living in different states will be subject to different state tax obligations. Often, the after-tax investment targets are roughly 20 percent to 25 percent lower than the before-tax investment targets, reflecting tax effects. For the public sector, it is usually enough to calculate before-tax project and equity rates of return.

### Applying Discounted Tax Flow to a Project after Rezoning

I will now apply the DCF pro forma analysis to the apartment project reviewed earlier but assuming the zoning has been changed. The next several tables are based on the "Apartment" tab in the Excel worksheet accompanying this book. The following inputs are made:

I use only the bottom-line total construction and land acquisition costs from table 3.2. The worksheet does not include an area for these details since actual development projects are so varied as to defy simplicity in worksheet design; yet, the output sections are robust enough to account for a wide range of development options. I also use all of the revenue information contained in table 3.2.

I assume a first-position mortgage for a 70 percent L/V ratio, at 6 percent over 30 years. The investors thus need to put $3.75 million of their own money into the project.

I further assume a 0.06 capitalization rate at project initiation but improving to 0.05 at the time of sale (both assumptions can be changed in the workbook). The reason for the improvement is that, as other redevelopment occurs in the area, the market not only stabilizes but it also attracts new development. In addition, if there is transit now or anticipated by the time of sale, the capitalization rate may improve as well. I also assume average annual rental income and expenses increasing at 3 percent annually, and 3 percent sales costs at sale after ten years.

Finally, I assume the investors need the following:

10 percent cash-on-cash return after the third year (the stabilization year)

12 percent average annual return for the total project (unleveraged return)

25 percent average annual return for the investors' equity (leveraged return).

Key results are reported in several tables, all of which are excerpted from the worksheet for this example and modified as needed for presentation here.

Table 3.5 reports the projected annual cash flow figures over the ten-year holding period. Based on the revenue and expenditure assumptions, net cash flow more than doubles from the first to the last year. However, the cash-on-cash never achieves the desired 10 percent target.

Table 3.6 shows the net sales proceeds. After paying off the loan balance and sales expenses, the investors pocket nearly $8.9 million. While this may seem like a handsome return for their $3.75 million equity investment, did they actually receive the overall return they need to justify this investment over other options? I will turn to this question next.

**Table 3.6.**
Net Sales Proceeds

| Project Value | Rate | Year 10 |
|---|---|---|
| Terminal cap rate | 5.00% | $14,789,604 |
| Net sales = Price less sales cost | 3.0% | $14,345,916 |
| Less mortgage balance | | ($5,491,876) |
| Net sales proceeds | | $8,854,040 |

Table 3.7 reports the unleveraged and leveraged returns after sale of the property. These returns include all of the cash flow received from the investment plus proceeds from its sale. The negative figures for Year 0 indicate the total project cost ($9.37 million) for the unleveraged analysis and the investors' equity ($3.75 million) for the leveraged analysis. For the unleveraged analysis, the sum of the stream of annual cash flow plus net sales proceeds comes to $15 million, but the IRR is 10.08 percent and the NPV is –$1.2 million. The leveraged analysis is similar; it shows total cash flow and net sales proceeds based only on the $3.75 million equity investment coming to nearly $9.1 million, resulting in an IRR of 15.73 percent and an NPV of nearly –$1.3 million. In effect, the investors lost money relative to opportunities they may have had elsewhere.

**Table 3.7.**
Unleveraged and Leveraged Return after Sale

| IRR—Unleveraged | Year 0 | Year 10 |
|---|---|---|
| Total investment | ($9,375,000) | |
| Project NOI | | $739,480 |
| Net sales price | | $14,345,916 |
| Total | ($9,375,000) | $15,085,396 |
| IRR—Project cost | | 10.08% |
| NPV—Project cost | | ($1,183,617) |
| **IRR—Leveraged** | **Year 0** | **Year 10** |
| Equity investment | ($3,750,000) | |
| Project cash flow | | $267,334 |
| Net proceeds | | $8,854,040 |
| Total | ($3,750,000) | $9,121,374 |
| IRR—Equity | | 15.73% |
| NPV—Equity | | ($1,343,209) |

*Note:* Intervening years have been excluded for brevity.

## Investment Decision

Recall that the equity investors need a 10 percent cash-on-cash return after the third year, a 12 percent unleveraged rate of return, and a 25 percent leveraged rate of return. Unfortunately, none of these targets were achieved even with the zoning change. If the community wants this project to proceed, a public-private partnership may be needed to make it work. How this may be accomplished is the subject of chapter 4.

# Chapter 4

# Survey of Public-Private Partnership Tools and the Role of Public Patient Equity to Leverage Private Real Estate Development

The public sector has many tools available to leverage private investment. Generally, they fall into planning and financing groups. This chapter begins with a review of planning tools but focuses on the suite of financial tools that are available to varying degrees to all local governments. It will show how the financing tools can improve investors' rates of return. The chapter concludes with a perspective on the role of public patient equity in leveraging private real estate development.

## Planning Tools

At its heart, redevelopment planning guides development to where it is desired and away from where it is not. Key planning tools include zoning, subdivision regulation, special area planning, and capital improvements programming.

All too often, desired development is stymied because of inadequate zoning and/or infrastructure. Zone changes and even wholesale amendments to zoning codes to allow desired development are often sufficient to leverage private sector investment. For instance, perhaps local government believes it can have affordable housing at a transit station at twenty units per acre but nothing happens. After studying the situation, it may find that land and improvement costs render this investment financially infeasible. It may be that changing zoning regulations to allow for sixty to eighty units per acre or so makes infill and redevelopment financially feasible.

Even if zoning is adequate, however, infrastructure may need to be upgraded. For instance, if water lines in the area are small and leak, they may not be able to accommodate new demands. Redevelopment plans should include an assessment of facility capacity to accommodate new development as well as a plan to use a combination of grants, debt financing, developer contributions, and other tools to upgrade infrastructure as needed.

## Financing Tools

Planning tools commonly are not enough to make the difference between having a desired project built by the private sector or not. Thankfully, local governments have several tools they can consider using to leverage desired private investment. These tools fall into the following categories:[1]

Cash flow support
Fee reductions
Cost shifting
Loan support
Tax credits
Land and air leases

Some tools—such as tax increment financing—can fall into two or more categories. Where that is the case, the tool will be described in detail in the most appropriate section with reference to its other applications. I use abbreviations for each of the tools in the workbook to help the user decide which tools may best apply to making a particular project financially feasible.

### Cash Flow Support

Often, a project would be financially feasible, especially in early years, but for cash flow needs until the project matures. The tools in this section provide short-term cash flow assistance. Tools in this category include, alphabetically:

Infrastructure reimbursement agreements (IRAs)
Property tax abatement (PTA)
Sales tax abatement (STA)

*Infrastructure reimbursement agreements (IRAs)*. Sometimes redevelopment needs infrastructure upgrades that substantially benefit the project itself, but the local government does not have the resources to pay for them. In these cases, P3 agreements can be structured so that the developer pays for those upgrades, but the local government gives the developer a portion of the property or sales taxes it pays to the government as a rebate. In a slightly different form, these agreements are also available as a cost-shifting tool.

*Property tax abatement (PTA)*. Many local communities may eliminate or reduce real and personal property taxes over a scheduled period as an incentive to new and expanding businesses. Usually, property tax abatement allows a property owner to phase in payment of property taxes over a designated period. Depending on state enabling legislation, this period may be any number of years between one and twenty or longer, with abatements usually ranging from 100 percent down to 10 percent for any given year. A variant of PTA is the infrastructure reimbursement agreements discussed above.

There are two limitations to abatement. First, it applies only to the property taxes relevant to the local jurisdiction. For instance, nationally, about half of property taxes go to local schools, a quarter to cities and/or counties, and the rest to special districts (but with wide variations among states and between local governments within the same state). If a city wishes to abate its share of property taxes to leverage real estate investment, the leveraging effect may be very small because local school districts, special districts, and other taxing jurisdictions may claim the vast majority of taxes. The workbook allows the user to input the applicable effective property tax rate to accurately apportion abatement.

Second, there cannot be property tax abatement combined with tax increment financing, for reasons that will be discussed in the cost-shifting section later.

Property tax abatement will increase net cash flow to the project equal to the taxes abated. As such, it will increase cash-on-cash, unleveraged, and leveraged returns, though perhaps not by much.

*Sales tax abatement (STA).* Some states allow local communities to eliminate or reduce sales taxes over a scheduled period as an incentive to new and expanding businesses. Usually, sales tax abatement allows a retail operation to phase in payment of sales taxes over a designated period. Depending on state enabling legislation, this period may be any number of years between one and usually no more than ten, though it could be longer, with abatements usually ranging from 100 percent down to 10 percent for any given year. Sometimes STA is used to offset capital investments made by the investor (see the discussion of tax increment financing and infrastructure reimbursement agreements).

Sales tax abatement has the same two limitations as property tax abatement: (1) it applies only to the sales taxes collected by the local government unit leveraging private investment, and (2) it cannot be used in tandem with tax increment financing.

Like property tax abatement, STA will increase net cash flow to the project equal to the taxes abated. Abatement will thus increase cash-on-cash, unleveraged, and leveraged returns somewhat.

In my view, local property and sales tax abatement is a relatively inexpensive way to leverage private investment. Though some may argue that local governments need the new revenues to cover new burdens imposed by new development, this may not be the case in most situations where abatement makes sense. Abatement should be allowed only in areas targeted for redevelopment based on a redevelopment plan. There will be occasions where infrastructure capacity exists to accommodate new development. For instance, redevelopment may not require any expansion to existing fire, police, library, general government, and education facilities or of the personnel operating them. In these cases, the impacts of new development will be zero or close to it. Technically, the marginal impact of the new development is at or near zero.

Moreover, if the abatement is successful in leveraging private investment in the target sites, there may be at least two collateral benefits. The new residents and workers will increase local spending, which will increase other local taxes and fees, perhaps in amounts greater than the abatement itself. Second, new residents will sustain new workers in support sectors (retail, medical, personal services, and so forth), who themselves may spend more money locally, especially if they live in the community. New workers hired through redevelopment may decide to buy or rent homes in the community, thereby adding to the local property and sales tax base.

Finally, abatement does not last forever. Eventually, the entire incremental property and sales tax revenues attributable to leveraged private investment will revert to the local government when the abatement period expires.

Let us consider the potential effect of property tax abatement on the apartment project. Suppose the effective property tax rate is 1 percent, which is just about the national average. (The property tax is applied to the market value of the development, not to what it costs.) Suppose also that the local government share of this is a quarter. Suppose further that the local government is willing to abate all of its share (100 percent) of property taxes for ten years. In the first year, property taxes are reduced by $23,615, rising to $30,812 in the tenth year as the property gains value.

To implement this in the apartment example worksheet, input 0.25 percent in the Local Property Tax Rate Available for abatement cell and 100 percent for all ten years in the PTA (%) cells. The property taxes abated are show n as revenue coming back to the project in the Plus: Property Tax Abatement line for all ten cash flow years. Table 4.1 shows the difference abatement can make to investors. While it is not enough to make the project financially feasible by itself, it is an important contribution.

**Table 4.1.**
Effect of Property Tax Abatement on Investment Performance

| Performance Measure | Target IRR | IRR before Abatement | IRR after Abatement | NPV before Abatement | NPV after Abatement |
|---|---|---|---|---|---|
| Cash-on-Cash after Year 3 | 10.00% | 4.49% | 5.48% | | |
| IRR—Unleveraged | 12.00% | 10.08% | 10.66% | ($1,183,617) | ($842,309) |
| IRR—Leveraged before Tax | 25.00% | 15.73% | 16.96% | ($1,343,209) | ($1,187,176) |

## Fee Reductions

Sometimes a relatively small reduction in front-end development costs is sufficient to make a project financially feasible. Three examples are provided here:

Fee waivers (FWs)

Utility fee reductions (UFRs)

Impact fee reductions (IFRs)

*Fee waivers (FW).* Local governments assess a wide range of fees to process new development. Collectively, they can account for up to 5 percent or more of the total construction costs. Waiver of fees, or their payment through such alternatives as Community Development Block Grant (CDBG) funds (see below), can reduce the cost.

Sometimes local governments will have targeted fee waiver policies so that development or redevelopment in targeted areas will be charged lower, or no, permitting and inspection fees. The lost revenue is covered by transfers from the general fund to ensure that the actual costs of permitting and inspecting are paid. One rationale for this approach is that redevelopment generates more economic and fiscal activity that will in effect reimburse the general fund for such transfers.

*Utility fee reductions (UFRs).* Many local governments charge connection fees to link new development to water and sewer services. They, too, can account for up to 5 percent or more of the total construction costs. Some local governments reduce or waive these fees for economic development, redevelopment, affordable housing, or other public policy purposes. Often, utilities are operated as self-financing enterprise accounts by local governments. As such, they have some flexibility to vary fees based on costs in specific areas of a community, such as those targeted for redevelopment.

*Impact fee reductions (IFRs).* Many local governments charge impact fees so that the impacts of new development on public facilities can be mitigated. They can also account for up to 5 percent or more of the total construction costs. Normally, impact fees must be paid to ensure legal defensibility, but they may be paid from such alternatives as CDBG funds or local housing or economic development funds or paid over time through a loan arrangement.

There are three important ways in which impact fees can be reduced to facilitate urban redevelopment. First, if infrastructure already substantially exists to serve redevelopment in a target service area, impact fees can be reduced to as low as zero. The theory is that where capacity exists, fees are not needed. This is in contrast to newly developing areas, which require new or expanded facilities. Tiering systems can be used to vary fees based on the extent to which existing facilities are adequate to meet the needs of new development, including redevelopment (Nelson, Bowles, et al. 2008).

The second way that impact fees can be reduced is by ensuring that they are based on the net new amount of development and not the total amount. The rehabilitation of a vacant 100,000-square-foot commercial building for commercial uses does not increase the total volume of development, so impact fees may not be assessed. If the rehabilitation includes an addition of 50,000 square feet, only the increment would be assessed impact fees. If the rehabilitation converted the 100,000 square feet into residential lofts, which collectively would have 25 percent more impact on facilities than would the building in commercial use, then the impact fees would be just 25 percent of the level otherwise assessed. One can imagine many nuances. The point is that local governments should be flexible in leveraging private investment in areas that are already developed, so adjusting impact fees to reflect the net change in impact is recommended (see Nelson, Bowles, et al. 2008).

The third adjustment can come when the developer can show that certain impacts will be less than the impact fee formula indicates. This is often the case with road or transportation impact fees that are based on the Institute of Transportation Engineers' *Trip Generation Manual* (2012). In central urban areas with transit options, for instance, Ewing and Hamidi (2014) estimate that road impacts associated with residential development can be up to half or less of similar residential development in newly developing suburban areas.

Let us assume that, of the $400,000 in permitting fees, which include utility connection and impact fees, half can be reduced through one or a combination of FW, UFR, and IFR options. For now, assume the reduction comes entirely from impact fee reductions based on reduced traffic impacts associated with its location. The effect is to reduce construction soft costs. In the apartment worksheet, put this figure into the Impact Fee Reductions (IFR) cell of the Leveraging Tools box. Because construction costs go down by $200,000, equity contributions also go down. The resulting performance measures are reported in table 4.2. Even though property tax abatement generated more savings over the entire ten-year holding period, the effect of a front-end reduction in equity requirements associated with fee reductions is about the same.

**Table 4.2.**
Effect of Fee Reductions on Investment Performance

| Performance Measure | Target IRR | IRR before Fee Reductions | IRR after Fee Reductions | NPV before Fee Reductions | NPV after Fee Reductions |
|---|---|---|---|---|---|
| Cash-on-Cash after Year 3 | 10.00% | 4.49% | 4.94% | | |
| IRR—Unleveraged | 12.00% | 10.08% | 10.39% | ($1,183,617) | ($983,617) |
| IRR—Leveraged before Tax | 25.00% | 15.73% | 16.72% | ($1,343,209) | ($1,143,209) |

## Cost Shifting

Shifting costs from the private developer to the public will require fulfillment of a public purpose. This was reviewed in chapter 2. Many government grant and related programs are available to cover substantial shares of the cost of such development. Some of these programs can be used to buy or write down the cost of land and to buy or write down the cost of building acquisition. Others can be used to pay for all or part of the cost of construction or rehabilitation of existing buildings. Still others can be used as "seed money" to cover the cost of feasibility studies, planning, loan packaging, and so forth—after all, the "soft" costs can be 10 percent or more of the entire project cost. There are also grants available to help pay for infrastructure costs and the costs of providing certain public services on a private site, such as public-access open spaces, arts and cultural elements, day care, and so forth.

The effect of all of these tools is to reduce project development costs and thus reduce the equity needed by investors. The following list of programs is not exhaustive and, while alphabetic, is in no particular order of prominence:

> Brownfield remediation (BR)
> Business improvement districts (BIDs)
> Capital recovery grants (CRGs)
> Community Development Block Grants (CDBGs)
> Congestion Mitigation and Air Quality Improvement (CMAQ) funds
> Economic Development Administration (EDA) grants
> Foundation grants (FGs)

General obligation bonds (GOBs)
Grant anticipation revenue (GARVEE) bonds
Infrastructure reimbursement agreements (IRAs)
Lease revenue bonds/certificates of participation (COPs)
Local improvement districts (LIDs): community improvement district; special assessment district; benefit assessment district; related
Parking districts (PDs)
Revenue bonds (RBs)
State infrastructure banks (SIBs)
Surface transportation program (STP)
Tax increment financing (TIF)
Transportation Infrastructure Finance and Innovation Act (TIFIA) grants
Urbanized area formula (UAF) program

*Brownfield remediation (BR).* The federal Environmental Protection Agency defines a brownfield as "a real property, the expansion, redevelopment, or reuse of which may be complicated by the presence or potential presence of a hazardous substance, pollutant, or contaminant."[2] This definition would seem to apply to a very large share of all redevelopment projects. The benefits of brownfield redevelopment include new private investment, which increases local tax revenues; land conservation, because development does not occur elsewhere; social benefits, such as redevelopment of blighted areas, thereby adding more local jobs and stabilizing communities; an elevation in nearby property values along with stimulating their redevelopment; and a general enhancement of economic revitalization and last but not least, environmental cleanup. Because of these and other benefits (see the introduction), federal and state agencies, and some local governments, provide grants, low-interest loans, and other services to undertake site assessment, environmental remediation, environmental remediation insurance, and associated engineering and legal costs. Public-private partnerships often have a public entity assume certain risks, which then leverages private investment.

*Business improvement districts (BIDs).* A business improvement district is a defined area within which businesses pay an additional tax or fee to fund improvements within the district's boundaries. Grant funds acquired by the city for special programs and/or incentives, such as tax abatements, can be made available to assist businesses or to recruit new business. There are other, similar improvement districts, including business improvement areas (BIAs), business revitalization zones (BRZs), community improvement districts (CIDs), special services areas (SSAs), and special improvement districts (SIDs).

Because terminology and powers vary by state, I review BIDs conceptually for their role in facilitating redevelopment. BIDs provide services, such as cleaning streets, providing security, making capital improvements, constructing pedestrian and streetscape enhancements, and marketing the area. The services provided by BIDs are supplemental to those already provided by the municipality. BIDs may generate revenue used to underwrite investments in new development. As in local improvement districts (LIDs), although property owners pay assessments, the BID improvements could be considered a grant when the assessments on any individual property are less than the cost of improvements investors would otherwise have to incur.

*Capital recovery grants (CRGs).* Sometimes, an entity will give a recoverable grant to leverage private investment and then wants the funds returned at sale of the property or after a certain number of years. These entities could include foundations, community development corporations, redevelopment authorities, other governmental agencies, or other donors. In many larger cities, affordable housing trust funds are generated from housing linkage fees (see Nelson, Nicholas, and Juergensmeyer (2008), state and federal sources (such as large financial settlements), local banks (perhaps through the Community Reinvestment Act process, which will be discussed later), foundations, and other sources. Sometimes these grants have declining amounts of recovery. For instance, if a development project is for a specific purpose, such as low-income housing, then for each year the project is occupied by a low-income household, the grant is reduced by a certain percentage until the balance becomes zero, at which point the operator may be able to repurpose the project.

*Community Development Block Grants (CDBGs).* The Community Development Block Grant (CDBG) program is one of the longest-running programs of the US Department of Housing and Urban Development. It funds local community development activities, such as affordable housing, antipoverty programs, and infrastructure development. CDBGs are subject to less federal oversight and are largely used at the discretion of the state and local governments and their subgrantees. They can be used for a variety of urban redevelopment activities, including covering a wide range of soft costs, finance infrastructure improvements, acquisition of land, and even helping build structures. Expenditures must be consistent with public-purpose findings.

*Congestion Mitigation and Air Quality Improvement (CMAQ) funds.* The CMAQ program was created under the Intermodal Surface Transportation Efficiency Act (ISTEA) of 1991, continued under the Transportation Equity Act for the 21st Century (TEA-21), and reauthorized by the Safe, Accountable, Flexible, Efficient Transportation Equity Act: A Legacy for Users (SAFETEA-LU). The purpose of the CMAQ program is to fund transportation projects or programs that will contribute to attainment or maintenance of the national ambient air quality standards (NAAQS) for ozone, carbon monoxide (CO), and particulate matter (PM). CMAQ funds may be used to establish new or expanded transportation projects or programs that reduce emissions, including capital investments in transportation infrastructure, congestion relief efforts, and other capital projects. For projects benefiting from redevelopment, expenditures may include transit system planning, design, and construction; construction of sidewalks connecting development to transit; construction of transit stations and platforms; and so forth.

*Economic Development Administration (EDA) grants.* The EDA is an agency in the US Department of Commerce that provides grants to economically distressed communities to generate new employment, help retain existing jobs, and stimulate industrial and commercial growth. These grants may be used to leverage private nonresidential development that generates jobs in economically distressed communities, including soft costs, land acquisition, and building construction.

*Foundation grants (FGs).* Foundations, especially those whose purpose is to advance the well-being of local communities, may be interested in providing grants or lower-interest loans. Grants are commonly used to cover soft costs and costs associated with land acquisition. Some foundations will also provide land and/or building write-down grants. The loan opportunities would be considered a form of loan support, which is discussed later.

*General obligation bonds (GOBs).* A general obligation bond is a common type of municipal bond that is secured by a state or local government's pledge to use legally available resources, including tax revenues, to repay bond holders. Most general obligation pledges at the local government level include a pledge to levy a property tax to meet debt service requirements, in which case holders of general obligation bonds have a right to compel the borrowing government to levy that tax to satisfy the local government's obligation. In the worst-case scenario, in which the local government cannot service bond debt, the bond holders can foreclose on public and even private property to pay off the bond, including payments in arrears. GOBs can be used for a wide range of purposes that benefit investment property, such as utilities, transportation, and sidewalks. To the extent that they are used to pay for things that the investors would have to finance otherwise, they can be considered an offset, usually against hard costs. Otherwise, bond payments made substantially by the benefiting development activity would be added to the operating costs of the project.

Qualifying GOBs are tax-exempt so that bond holders (those who lend money through buying bonds) earn interest free from federal taxes as well as state taxes in the state where it was issued (in which case the bond is called double tax-exempt). This allows the borrowing agency to pay less interest. For instance, suppose a bond holder is in the 40 percent combined state and federal tax marginal bracket. If a non-tax-exempt bond yielded 5.0 percent the after-tax yield would be 3.0 percent or 40 percent less. It is the 3.0 percent rate that the tax exempt bond would cost the issuer. In this way, not only are costs shifted away from the benefiting development to the larger pool of tax payers but the interest paid is also less.

*Grant anticipation revenue (GARVEE) bonds.* GARVEE bonds are a special type of bond issued by a state or a state infrastructure bank under federal guidelines. States must repay the bonds using federal funds expected to be received in the future. Federal guidelines state that "an eligible debt financing instrument is a bond, note, certificate, mortgage, lease, or other debt financing instrument issued by a state or political subdivision of a state or a public authority, the proceeds of which are used to fund a project eligible for assistance under Title 23." GARVEE bonds may be used for major projects receiving federal funding. They can be considered a grant against hard costs to investors if the investors otherwise would have had to improve portions of major highways fronting their project.

*Infrastructure reimbursement agreements (IRAs).* There are occasions when local government cannot finance the facility improvements needed to leverage private investment. In these situations, the investors may be willing to finance the improvements provided they are reimbursed through the local share of property and/or sales tax abatements. Another alternative is to have local government assess subsequent nearby new development a proportionate share of its cost of facility improvements through a "late-comer" fee.

*Lease revenue bonds (LRBs)/certificates of participation (COPs).* Lease revenue bonds are a variant of revenue bonds. The revenue stream backing the bond is created from lease payments made by a public agency using the structure that is developed. Often, a private financing entity builds the facility, issues financing bonds, and retains title to the facility until the debt is retired. LRBs do not require voter approval.

Certificates of participation are a variation in which an investor buys a share in the improvements or infrastructure the government entity intends to fund. This contrasts with a bond, in which the investor loans the government or municipality money to make these improvements. This is used primarily when the government or municipality has a charter-mandated debt ceiling.

Where the tool generates revenue to finance improvements, it may be considered a form of long-term financing. Where it generate funds to build a facility for a public purpose and the tenant, such as a government entity, retires the debt through lease payments, it may be considered a grant for construction, but rent revenue pledged to the lease must be reduced from cash flow available to the investor.

*Local improvement districts (LIDs): community improvement district; special assessment district; benefit assessment district; related.* These are mechanisms for property owners with common concerns to band together and assess themselves for purely local improvements, such as sidewalk repair, neighborhood park rehabilitation, streets, and so forth. They must be authorized by state law and follow specific state procedures for formation, governance, and the issuance of bonds to finance the projects. They are funded through such sources as general taxes, special assessments, or fees based on formulas (such as street frontage). Although property owners pay assessments, the LID improvements could be considered a grant when the assessments on any individual property are less than the cost of improvements investors would have to incur otherwise. (See also *business improvement districts.*)

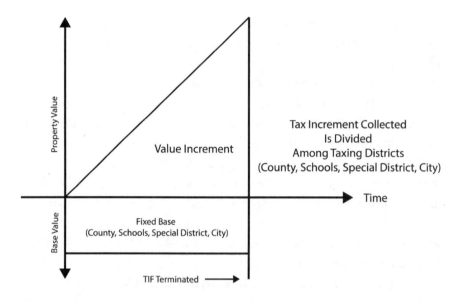

**Figure 4.1.** Tax increment finance. (In the public domain; adapted from the Wisconsin Department of Finance)

*Parking districts (PDs).* These are a variant of the local improvement district but focus on providing parking, usually for downtowns and suburban centers. A revenue bond is used to finance the capital construction while parking fees retire the debt and help with maintenance. Sometimes a BID will underwrite the revenue bond and use parking revenues for operations and maintenance. Parking districts can shift the cost of providing expensive decked or underground parking from an investment project to a larger pool of properties. To investors, a parking structure built and maintained through a parking district can be considered a grant if it reduces the costs of building parking for the development project.

*Revenue bonds (RBs).* A revenue bond is a special type of municipal bond distinguished by its guarantee of repayment solely from revenues generated by a specified revenue-generating entity associated with the purpose of the bonds, rather than from a tax. Unlike general obligation bonds (see below), only the revenues specified in the legal contract between the bond holder and the bond issuer are required to be used for repayment of the principal and interest of the bonds; other revenues (notably tax revenues) and the general credit of the issuing agency are not so encumbered. Because the pledge of security is not as great as that of general obligation bonds, revenue bonds may carry a slightly higher interest rate than GOBs; however, they are usually considered the second most secure type of municipal bonds. For redevelopment purposes, revenue bonds may be issued for projects that generate revenue from public gatherings (such as conferences, conventions, civic and cultural events) the development of which can stimulate other development in the area. To the extent that revenue bonds finance improvements that would otherwise have to be paid by investors (such as street, sidewalk, utility, and related improvements), they can be considered an offset against relevant soft and hard costs. As with the case of GOBs, bond payments made substantially by the benefiting development activity would be added to the operating costs of the project. Moreover, they can also be tax exempt, though the tax rules are more rigorous. Bond attorneys will be helpful in navigating tax exemption considerations.

*State infrastructure banks (SIBs).* The SIB program gives states the capacity to lower the borrowing costs of their transportation investments and to leverage federal transportation financing resources. A SIB, much like a private bank, can offer a range of loans and credit enhancement opportunities to public and private sponsors of Title 23 highway construction projects or Title 49 transit capital projects. By offering SIB support for a project, the state may be able to attract private, local government, and additional state financial resources, leveraging a small amount of SIB assistance into a larger dollar investment. SIB capital can also be used as collateral to borrow in the bond market or to establish a guaranteed reserve fund. When these funds are used to finance transportation improvements investors would otherwise have to pay for, they can be considered a grant for the project.

*Surface Transportation Program (STP).* The STP provides flexible funding that may be used by state and local governments for projects on any federal-aid highway, including the National Highway System, bridge projects on any public road, transit capital projects, and intra- and inter-city bus terminals and facilities. Expenditures under this program can include all those under CMAQ funds.

*Tax increment financing (TIF).* TIF is a financing tool that allows local governments to invest in infrastructure and other improvements and to finance those investments by capturing property and/or sales tax revenue from the newly developed property.[3] Under laws in all states enabling this technique, an area is identified as a tax increment finance district[4] and designated for certain types of development to facilitate implementation of a redevelopment plan for the area. Conceptually, "but for" this public action, private redevelopment will not be efficient. As redevelopment occurs and property values rise, the incremental property and/or sales tax paid on that private development is used to pay for the improvements that made the private redevelopment possible. To be effective, however, all jurisdictions that have a claim on those taxes must agree to the TIF funding system. The property tax version of TIF is illustrated in figure 4.1 but can easily be extended to a sales tax version.

When a tax increment finance district is created, the then-existing value of all the taxable property within it is established. The taxes continue to be collected on the base value and distributed after the district is formed in the same proportion as before. Until the district is terminated (usually when any bonds financed from TIF revenues are retired), the incremental property (or sales) taxes generated from new taxable investment are dedicated to financing improvements, often providing debt service.

TIF funds can be used to assemble land, upgrade infrastructure, demolish structures, clean up contaminated soils, build or expand transportation improvement roads, upgrade water, wastewater, or drainage systems, and so forth. They can also be used for expenses relating to planning and financing improvements. Finally, they can be used for public-purpose portions of private property, such as public gathering places (including the lobbies of buildings), day care centers, museums, and so forth. Like GOBs, TIF bonds can be tax-exempt. There are strict Internal Revenue Service rules and rules in each of the states relating to tax treatment of TIF bonds.

*Transportation Infrastructure Finance and Innovation Act (TIFIA) grants.* The TIFIA program provides federal credit assistance to nationally or regionally significant surface transportation projects, including highway, transit, and rail systems. The program is designed to fill market gaps and to leverage substantial private co-investment by providing projects with supplemental or subordinate debt. To the extent that this program finances transportation improvements the investors would have to incur anyway, they can be considered a grant against soft and hard costs.

*Urbanized Area Formula (UAF) program.* The UAF makes federal resources available to urbanized areas and to governors for transit capital and operating assistance in urbanized areas and for transportation-related planning. Activities include planning, engineering design, and evaluation of transit projects and other technical transportation-related studies. As with TIFA, to the extent that this program finances transportation improvements the investors would have to incur anyway, they can be considered a grant against soft and hard costs.

Suppose that the subject apartment building is in an area where local governments and other organizations want to redevelop as well as increase the number of residents. Without some assistance, this may not be possible. Suppose that $100,000 is generated each from CDBG funds to cover soft costs (add this to the Leveraging Tools box in the accompanying worksheet), a LID to cover sidewalk and drainage improvements, and a CRG (based on the local government housing development trust fund) to cover part of the land acquisition costs. Table 4.3 shows the effect of these forms of grants, totaling $300,000, on investment performance measures. In all cases, performance improves mostly because investor equity contributions are reduced at the front end.

**Table 4.3.**
Effect of Grants and Capital Investment Offsets on Investment Performance

| Performance Measure | Target IRR | IRR before Grants | IRR after Grants | NPV before Grants | NPV after Grants |
|---|---|---|---|---|---|
| Cash-on-Cash after Year 3 | 10.00% | 5.24% | 6.75% | | |
| IRR—Unleveraged | 12.00% | 8.64% | 11.51% | ($1,744,152) | ($283,617) |
| IRR—Leveraged before tax | 25.00% | 11.52% | 21.07% | ($1,769,896) | ($443,209) |

# Loan Support

Mezzanine financing—the bridge between senior debt and equity investors—is often expensive—so much so that it can make real estate investments financially infeasible. One solution is for the public sector to provide some of this form of financing. While private mezzanine financiers require a much higher rate than senior debt, the public sector rate can actually be lower than senior lenders because of their public-purpose orientation and because their interest earnings are tax-free as government or nonprofit organizations. They are not a replacement for the magnitude of senior debt, however, as they are restricted in both the base of funds available for this purpose and the need to be sure they are used for public purposes based on redevelopment plans. A sampling of these below-market loan support programs includes the following:

Community development corporations (CDCs)
Community Reinvestment Act (CRA)
Low-interest loans (LILs)
Public development authorities (PDAs)
Private activity bonds (PABs)
Revolving loan funds (RLFs)

*Community development corporations (CDCs).* CDCs are private non-profit organizations incorporated to advance community development through providing programs, services, and activities. CDCs usually serve specific geographic areas, such as neighborhoods or cities. They often serve lower-income households or economically distressed neighborhoods. Their activities can include economic development, education, community organizing and advocacy, and real estate development. CDCs are often associated with the development of affordable housing and are commonly funded by foundations and private gifts. An emerging source of revenue for many is acquiring land through gifts or property tax foreclosures and working with banks under the Community Reinvestment Act (see below) to provide below-market construction and permanent home finance loans to targeted low-income households. The CDCs keep the land, so home ownership is through a land lease with the CDC receiving a small land lease payment from the household. Because CDCs are nonprofit, loans they make can be considered below-market loans.

*Community Reinvestment Act (CRA).* The CRA encourages federally regulated banks to help meet the needs of borrowers in communities where they operate, especially those in low- and moderate-income neighborhoods. The law was passed in 1977 to reduce discriminatory credit practices against buying homes in low-income neighborhoods, which is known as redlining. Since then, research has shown that the CRA has increased credit access to low- and moderate-income borrowers (Barr 2005). While the law does not require lend-ers to provide below-market loans, many do nonetheless when they partner with local CDCs, PDAs, and other governmental and nonprofit organizations.

*Low-interest loans (LILs).* Local governments may have access to funds that can be used to provide below-market loans for all or part of an investment. If it is just for part, it is often used for mezzanine financing. Nonprofits and foundations may also be sources. (See *public development authorities* and *community development corporations.*)

*Public development authorities (PDAs).* PDAs have numerous purposes, but they tend to focus on planning and implementing redevelopment plans for local governments. Depending on state enabling authorities, they may have the power to condemn land, to sell it to private parties, and to incur debt and finance debt. Debt is usually financed from the additional taxes generated from the increased assessed value of the property (see *tax increment financing*). PDAs support themselves in several ways, such as from local government budgets, debt proceeds, tax incremental district assessments, and proceeds from sales of assets. As tax-exempt organizations that can use the credit rating of local governments, they can borrow money at rates from one-third to one-half low-er than the private sector. PDAs are thus an important source of low-interest loans for redevelopment purposes.

*Private activity bonds (PABs).* This is a form of tax-exempt municipal bond in which a local government entity is seeking to raise money for a private compa-ny. A local government issues a private activity bond when it wants to attract a business and the jobs it brings to the area, especially when the business may be otherwise unable to obtain financing for the project. To qualify for tax-exempt status, the local government issuing the bond must be able to prove that a public benefit derives from the private activity bond. Private activity bonds generally are not guaranteed by the local government, so the collateral is the borrower's assets. This often results in higher risk to the lender and therefore higher payments to the investor. Moreover, there are strict rules as to which projects qualify.

*Revolving loan funds (RLFs).* These are self-replenishing pools of money through which interest and principal payments on current or retired loans are used to issue new ones. RLFs provide access to capital lending for development and other purposes. While RLFs must generate enough interest to replenish the fund for future loans, because proceeds are usually tax-free (when managed by a government or nonprofit agency), the interest charged can be below market. The funds' initial capital can come from many sources, including direct appropriations from state or local government; banks and other lending institutions, especially when combined with the Community Reinvestment Act (see above); utility companies; and private foundations. Federal sources, which often contain restrictions on the activities for which loans are made, include Community Development Block Grants (HUD), the Community Adjustment and Investment Program (USDA), the Economic Adjustment Assistance Program (EDA), and the Brownfields Revolving Loan Fund (EPA).

Suppose the investors are able to secure a low-interest loan for their apartment building equivalent to 10 percent of the L/V ratio, or $937,500. Also suppose it is at 3 percent amortized over thirty years. Table 4.4 shows the effect of this leveraging tool on performance measures. Notice that the leveraged returns increase substantially over the other options. Because the loan will be paid back, the lending entity can recycle the money to other ventures; it also earns interest on the arrangement, though perhaps just covering its borrowing costs (I will discuss this in the conclusion). However, because total debt service is increased, the cash-on-cash return remains low.

**Table 4.4.**
Effect of a 10 Percent Low-Interest Loan at 3 Percent and a Thirty-Year Period on Investment Performance

| Performance Indicator | Target IRR | IRR before Low-Interest Second | IRR after Low-Interest Second | NPV before Low-Interest Second | NPV after Low-Interest Second |
|---|---|---|---|---|---|
| Cash-on-cash after Year 3 | 10.00% | 5.24% | 4.36% | | |
| IRR—Unleveraged | 12.00% | 8.64% | 10.08% | ($1,744,152) | ($1,183,617) |
| IRR—Leveraged before tax | 25.00% | 11.52% | 19.05% | ($1,769,896) | ($651,583) |

## Tax Credits

The last group of financial tools that can facilitate private redevelopment are tax credits. Many states incentivize certain kinds of real estate and economic development (see Story 2012).[5] However, my focus here is on federal programs because they apply to all states. Unlike a tax deduction that merely reduces taxable income, a tax credit returns qualified taxes. Such credits include the following:

Low/Moderate Income Housing Tax Credits (LIHTCs)
Historic Preservation Tax Credits (HPTCs)
New Market Tax Credits (NMTCs)

*Low/Moderate Income Housing Tax Credits (LIHTCs).* The federal Low/Moderate Income Housing Tax Credit (typically denoted as LIHTC and often pronounced "lie-tech") program is a dollar-for-dollar tax credit provided to investors of affordable housing projects.[6] It was created under the Tax Reform Act of 1986 and has become the nation's most successful low/moderate-income housing program. Between 1987 and 2010, more than 2.2 million units were built, or more than 100,000 units in more than 1,400 projects per year. In 2012, the LIHTC program gave each state the equivalent of about $2.25 per resident in tax credit authority for the acquisition, rehabilitation, and/or new construction of rental housing targeted to low- and moderate-income households, defined as earning less than 50 percent or less than 60 percent of the area median income (AMI; usually the metropolitan or micropolitan statistical area), respectively.

The unique feature of the program is that LIHTCs cover up to 90 percent of the cost of new or rehabilitated structure value (land is excluded) and up to 30 percent for the value of an existing structure (also excluding land), spread over ten years.[7] Suppose a new rental apartment structure costs $10 million to build and all the units are contracted for low/moderate-income households. The annual credit would be $900,000. However, the actual credit would be negotiated between the developer and the state or local housing finance agency administering the program.

To take immediate advantage of the tax credits, syndications of investors have been formed to buy them at a discount. If the discount is 10 percent, the developer gets 90 percent of the maximum $9 million in credits at the front end rather than waiting over ten years to receive all of the credits, or $8.1 million.[8] This would be considered a grant to the developer. Because the developer can also borrow money against the project with the debt retired from rental income, the tax credits become an instant windfall. In practice, because rental revenue is reduced, the actual building value is less and so it would be a commercial loan.

In return for the credit, the developer and subsequent owners must agree to rent the subsidized units to low- and/or moderate-income households for at least fifteen years, and their rents cannot exceed 30 percent of the AMI for their income bracket. States are free to extend this period, however, and many do. Utah, for instance, requires a minimum contract of forty years, and despite this there are more applications annually than there are credits to award. In contrast, Georgia uses the federal minimum, which essentially means that after fifteen years, these low-rent units revert to market-rate units, which reduces the overall supply of low-income housing.

State and local agencies administering the program can also encourage LIHTC projects to be located in redevelopments, transit stations, or other areas. For instance, Utah awards extra points in competitive LIHTC bids for projects located within one-third mile of a rail transit station. The result is that in recent years most of Utah's LIHTC projects have been built in those locations.

*Historic Preservation Tax Credits (HPTCs)*. Under this program, an owner of rental/income-producing property listed by the National Park Service's Register of National Historic Places (or properties that are contributing resources within a National Register Historic District) may be eligible for a 20 percent investment tax credit for the rehabilitation of the historic structure. The rehabilitation may include commercial, industrial, or residential rental property. In addition, the tax incentive program allows for a 10 percent tax credit for rehabilitation of nonhistoric, nonresidential buildings built before 1936. These credits can be claimed for the year in which expenses were incurred. However, as the credits cannot exceed 30 percent of the taxes that would be paid, they are sometimes sold to syndicates at a discount, which allows the developer to maximize credits at the front end.

*New Markets Tax Credits (NMTCs)*. The New Markets Tax Credit (NMTC) program was established in 2000 as part of the Community Renewal Tax Relief Act of 2000. Its goal is to induce revitalization of low-income and distressed communities. The NMTC program provides tax credit incentives to investors for equity investments for qualified organizations investing in low-income communities. The credit equals 39 percent of the investment, paid out as 5 percent in each of the first three years and then 6 percent in the final four years. Like the LIHTC program, syndicators can buy the credits at a discount, thereby providing the developer with a front-end grant.

Suppose the project was awarded New Markets Tax Credits based on soft and hard construction costs (land being excluded), and the credits were sold to a syndicate, netting $1.5 million to the developer. Table 4.5 shows the effect on investment performance. Here we see that all investment targets are achieved. Obviously, New Markets and LIHTC tax credits are attractive to investors; however, because of this, competition for credits is substantial and often leads to a combination of concessions and reduced availability of credits. These grants are also competitive, so they cannot be relied upon. This is especially the case with the LIHTC program.

**Table 4.5.**
Effect of New Markets Tax Credit on Investment Performance

| Performance Indicator | Target IRR | IRR before Tax Credits | IRR after Tax Credits | NPV before Tax Credits | NPV after Tax Credits |
|---|---|---|---|---|---|
| Cash-on-Cash after Year 3 | 10.00% | 5.24% | 9.84% | | |
| IRR—Unleveraged | 12.00% | 8.64% | 12.57% | ($1,744,152) | $316,383 |
| IRR—Leveraged before tax | 25.00% | 11.52% | 26.77% | ($1,769,896) | $156,791 |

*Note*: Tax credit applied to soft and hard costs only, with a net return of 90 percent of the 39 percent credit awarded.

# Criteria for Choosing the Tools to Leverage Private Redevelopment

As we have seen, private redevelopment can be leveraged in many ways. Usually, one tool is not sufficient. While tax credit programs can leverage private redevelopment, there are typically more applicants than awardees. In this section, I present my criteria for choosing tools to leverage private redevelopment. Above all, redevelopment needs to be consistent with local plans. In those cases, tools authorized for redevelopment require plans as their rationale for implementation.

However, changes in planning and land-use controls may not be enough. If the local public development authority wants this project to proceed, it may have to help financially. But how does it know which tools are the most prudent? While every project will be different, I offer three principles for using public resources to leverage private real estate investment:

1. Explore the availability of federal tax credit programs. These programs cost local governments little, if anything. The tax credit allocations are based on federal, state, and sometimes local policies, including the requirement to be consistent with local land-use regulations. Allocations are also based on high levels of scrutiny guided by federal and state rules so there is important external oversight. Still, tax credit projects will usually account for a very small share of redevelopment opportunities.

2. Use those financial tools that leave local government the least vulnerable to losses if the project fails. I thus recommend using property and sales tax abatement, fee reductions or waivers, and infrastructure reimbursement agreements (from project-related property and/or sales taxes). The rationale is that, while local government could lose those revenues, they are probably a very small share of the local revenue base and are likely easier to recover than other potential losses, thus minimizing local-government risk. For instance, if a grant is given, it should be the smallest amount needed to make the project feasible and, if the project fails, the local government should have recourse to the project's assets. There are examples where a developer requested local government grants to build residential units in redevelopment areas and received them without local government analysis to determine the appropriate size of the grant. The result was that many developers received far higher rates of return (more than 40 percent in one case) than the prevailing market. In addition, the local governments had less money available to leverage new projects. The same should be the case with loans; local government needs to provide only the amount of loans needed to make the project financially feasible and no more, in order to have money available to leverage other projects. This advice holds for nondebt local government resources.

3. Only use debt financing for a principal benefit of a specific development project after exploring all other options. Debt financing should be used for large-scale redevelopment from which many projects can benefit. In

this situation, the failure of one or a few projects may be offset by the success of others.

Given these principles, how can the example apartment project be made financially feasible? Assume that tax credits are not an option. Suppose the local government combined property tax abatement at 100 percent of the municipal property taxes for ten years, $200,000 in fee reductions, $300,000 in cost-shifting measures, and a $1.6 million loan at a rate of 3 percent paid over thirty years. Table 4.6 shows the effect on investment performance. In the case of cash-on-cash and leveraged returns, the investors reach their target returns, and nearly so for unleveraged returns. While the debt coverage ratio falls out of range—to 1.13 compared to the target of 1.25—this is only because of the higher debt associated with mezzanine financing; the senior debt remains well secured with a DCF of more than 1.25 for its purposes.

**Table 4.6.**
Effect of the Use of Local Government Leveraging Tools on Investment Performance*

| Performance Indicator | Target IRR | IRR before Leveraging | IRR after Leveraging | NPV before Leveraging | NPV after Leveraging |
|---|---|---|---|---|---|
| Cash-on-Cash after Year 3 | 10.00% | 5.24% | 10.28% | | |
| IRR—Unleveraged | 12.00% | 8.64% | 11.43% | ($1,744,152) | ($83,617) |
| IRR—Leveraged before tax | 25.00% | 11.52% | 32.98% | ($1,769,896) | $157,626 |

*Property tax abatement, selected fee reductions (such as lower impact fees attributable to lower traffic impacts), small locally generated grant, and small locally supplied loan.

It is often the case that only some investment targets are achieved through a DCF analysis. From the perspective of local planners, economic development professionals, public officials, and engaged citizens, the most important target is the unleveraged return. Those actors in the P3 process cannot know the equity or tax implications of the investors, nor should they. Their principal aim should be to achieve the most objective investment benchmark, which is the unleveraged return based on the total project investment.

Other types of investors may put more weight on the unleveraged return. These would include long-term institutional investors who may buy projects without debt financing, such as real estate investment trusts, pension funds, insurance companies, and foundations. If the investors and the local govern-ment want to hit all three targets, they may engage in negotiation to find a more precise mix of locally available leveraging options to do so.

## Case Study: Redevelopment in Hillsboro, Oregon

Figures 4.2a and 4.2b show before-and-after redevelopment of a 1.1-acre site in Hillsboro, Oregon. Hillsboro—a suburb about twenty miles west of downtown Portland—provides an example of a redevelopment plan com-bined with public efforts to facilitate desirable redevelopment. Fregonese Associates of Portland, Oregon, to whom I am indebted for this case study, and John Southgate, who was the economic development director in Hill-sboro at the time, were actively engaged in the redevelopment planning process.

In the early 2010s, the City of Hillsboro and the metropolitan plan-ning organization (the federally chartered transportation planning and funding agency) for the region, called Metro, engaged in a redevelop-ment planning process and entered into a development agreement with a private firm to construct a mixed-use building on a 1.1-acre site within a transit-oriented development (TOD) served by the region's light rail system.

The site is located at the intersection of Fourth Street and Main Street in downtown Hillsboro, which has evolved from being a Main Street typical of rural, agriculture-serving towns through the 1950s, to a typ-ically declining suburban Main Street through the 1990s as shopping centers diverted economic activity away from it, to a reviving Main Street facilitated by a redevelopment plan and using public resources to leverage private redevelopment. The 1.1-acre site itself is the home of a 5,084-square-foot bank, initially with only lobby services and later with a drive-through option. The FAR for the site was about 0.12, with 88 per-cent of the site paved and used mostly for parking. The investors antici-pate that the renovated bank building will become a brew pub or similar business to help achieve the redevelopment plan's objective to create an "18-hour" Main Street district.

**Figure 4.2a.** Redevelopment site at Fourth and Main Streets in downtown Hillsboro, Oregon. The 1.1-acre site included a mid-twentieth-century bank (on the right), a drive-through (left), and extensive parking (behind). (Credit: Tokola Properties)

**Figure 4.2b.** Nearing completion in 2014, the main bank building (far right) was preserved and converted into retail space, and seventy-one residential units with ground-floor retail were constructed on drive-through lanes and most of the parking. Parking access is behind the buildings. (Credit: Tokola Properties)

The redevelopment investment is consistent with the City's Main Street redevelopment plan, which includes such elements as (1) strengthening and sustaining community (in this case by expanding housing supply and options); (2) enhancing neighborhoods and districts (in this case by adding more mixed land uses); (3) preserving the environment (such as by preventing more development on the urban fringe; (4) creating economic opportunity (in this case by adding more and a wider range of jobs; and (5) promoting health and safety (in this case by reducing vehicle miles traveled per person, which improves air quality and traffic safety).

One outcome of the process was changes to the development code to (1) allow for more residential density (ninety units per acre instead of thirty-six), (2) eliminate minimum parking for all uses except residential, which was reduced from 1.5 stalls per unit to 0.75; (3) eliminate the prohibition on ground-floor residential use in a commercial area; and (4) eliminate minimum lot size, width, and depth. This allowed the TOD area to be developed without any variances.

Several local public partner tools were used to facilitate the redevelopment of this site, including the following:

- Property tax abatement on the residential units for 60 percent of their market value
- A grant of $150,000 in predevelopment contributions from the city and Metro, the metropolitan planning organization, which was matched at $75,000 from the developer
- A land write down from the city and Metro (they jointly acquired the site in 1998 for about $660,000, it was appraised in 2011 for more than $1 million, and it was sold to the developer for $150,000)
- An easement from Metro to allow development on its land, which was valued at $465,000 (the easement is tied to the induced transit ridership associated with the development)
- Paying $870,000 of about $1.1 million in impact fees over ten

years by the local urban renewal agency
- A complex arrangement to remediate brownfield contamination as follows—the city negotiated acquisition of the property "as is," based in part on what proved an initial but unreliable Level 2 environmental assessment, so this had the city turn to Metro to cover about 90 percent of the purchase price; however, the city indemnified Metro for future environmentally related costs. After a full environmental assessment, the developer removed partially contaminated soil to enable below-grade parking, the cost of which was covered in part by $100,000 provided from Metro to the city and by the city borrowing $300,000 from a state environmental remediation fund to be repaid over time by its urban renewal agency.

The overall P3 agreement resulted in a $16 million redevelopment project comprising seventy-one market-rate apartments, of which eight are ground-floor live-work units; 3,900 square feet of ground-floor retail space, which will help the Main Street District become an eighteen-hour center of activity; 6,000 square feet of a rehabilitated mid-twentieth-century bank; and seventy-one below-grade access-restricted parking spaces for the apartments plus thirty surface-level spaces serving the retail activities.

In all, about $2 million of a variety of local public partner investments were used to leverage $16 million in private real estate development. Not only were jobs created and housing provided, but the project is seen as a catalyst for other private real estate development along Main Street, most of which needs little if any public partner resources.

As can be seen, this 1.1-acre redevelopment was complex. Over time, the city will generate more local tax and fee revenues from the development than all of the local costs incurred. In addition, other costs are avoided, such as installing new infrastructure in greenfield locations farther away at lower density, and unlikely with the economic return the redeveloped site generates.

# The Role of Public Patient Equity to Leverage Private Investment

The development plan needs to be implemented by a public development agency (PDA), which can be known by several different names. The PDA can be part of the local government (such as the planning department or housed within the city/county manager's office) or a public redevelopment authority established under state enabling legislation. The PDA would use all of the planning, consultation, legal, and financing powers outlined in the plan to implement it.

A key function of the PDA is to use financial resources to leverage private redevelopment. Depending on the situation, either directly because the PDA has the authority or indirectly in partnership with other local government agencies, these local financial resources include tax abatement, fee waivers, CDBG funds, resources from LIDs and BIDs, issuing bonds, and providing grants and low-interest loans. The PDA can also assist in packaging and combining resources to leverage federal and state grants and New Markets Tax Credits.

PDAs, however, have their own bills to pay. While many receive funding from local government and can recover their costs of processing grants and loans from those activities, many other PDAs need to become financial partners with the private sector. Indeed, while the public sector provides direct support for private real estate investment, it also incurs the risk of losing its investment. In effect, whether formal or not, the public sector becomes a partner in a P3. This has the advantage of giving both parties the incentive to make a project succeed. Christopher B. Leinberger (2001, 2007) calls on public entities to invest *patient equity* into targeted public-private partnership real estate developments, especially redevelopment projects. I will review how patient equity works, apply it to a sample investment, and review the special case of public financing of parking structures as a form of patient equity to leverage large-scale private redevelopment.

## Patient Equity Foundations

Patient equity is added to the real estate capital stack. Recall from chapter 3 that the capital stack comprises (1) senior debt ranging from about

60 percent to 80 percent of project costs commanding returns of 2.50 to 4.00 percentage points (250 to 400 basis points) above the prime lending rate; (2) mezzanine financing, which can include debt and equity interests ranging roughly the difference between the senior debt and 80 percent to 95 percent of total project costs with returns of 2.00 to 3.00 percentage points (200 to 300 basis points) higher than senior debt; and (3) equity investment covering the rest of the project costs and commanding returns of about 20 percent to 30 percent. There are times when government agencies and occasionally nonprofit organizations contribute to the development in ways that are reviewed later in this section. When they do so, public agencies should not give their resources away (in the form of grants and tax abatements and such) but, rather, take a "patient" equity position in the project.

Under Leinberger's patient equity scheme, each "tranche," or slice, which Leinberger uses here to describe all investment positions above senior debt, has its own ownership position and agreements on payment terms, including timing of payment and yield on investment. Figure 4.3 illustrates first, second, and third tranches. The first tranche is conventional mezzanine financing, while the second tranche is the traditional equity position. The third tranche belongs to the public sector, reflecting its contributions to leverage private real estate investment. Where senior debt and the first two tranches are equal to 100 percent of project costs, the resources marshaled by the public sector to leverage private real estate development are added so that total financing is greater than 100 percent.

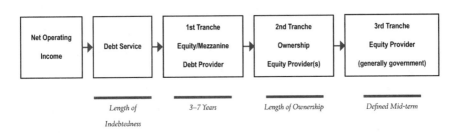

**Figure 4.3.** Time frame of return to tranches. *Source*: Adapted from Christopher B. Leinberger (2007).

## Patient Equity Applications

There are several ways in which patient equity can be invested and returned. Here is a list of common forms:

Capital recovery grants (CRGs)
Cash throw-off (CTO)
Debt financing (DF)
Land leases (LLs)
Air rights leases (ARLs)
Share of net sales price (Sale)

*Capital recovery grants (CRGs).* This tool was reviewed earlier in this chapter, but instead of an outright grant, the funds may be recovered very late in a project's investment period, perhaps even to the point where it is sold or refinanced.

*Cash throw-off (CTO).* Income-producing projects may be asked to provide a portion of the income to the PDA; this is called a cash throw-off. Normally, the PDA and the developer would enter into an agreement resulting in the developer paying the PDA a share of the cash flow from the project. There are many ways to do this, such as through level payments (perhaps escalated annually in relation to rent escalation), percentages of EGI or NOI, or another formula. In the workbook, the analyst would assume a level payment.

*Debt financing (DF).* As reviewed in chapter 2, PDAs often have the ability to make below-market loans to qualifying parties. The interest charged can include a small increment to generate cash flow back to the PDA, in addition to the interest needed to finance the debt it incurred for the deal.

*Land leases (LL).* Under a land lease, publicly owned land is rented to a real estate development entity who then builds structures and generates revenue. Part of the revenue is used to make the land lease payments. Land lease contracts often range from about fifty to ninety-nine years. When the lease is nearing expiration, the landowner and lessee often renegotiate lease terms so that both can continue a financially favorable relationship. Land lease contracts, especially where the public sector owns the land, usually require that the property be developed in ways meeting public sector benefits such as parks or plazas, public building spaces such as for museums or libraries, affordable housing, and space for nonprofit organizations.

Land leases can reduce investor development cost by up to the price of the land. If a project will cost $5 million and the land share would have been $1 million, the project cost can be reduced by up to this amount. Of course, the land lease usually results in rental payments, so that will have the effect of reducing the rate of return, but the lease payments could be structured to achieve the target return. The structure could include very low or no payments in early years, increasing in later years as the project's revenues grow.

Land leases are especially effective in transitioning areas and closer-in urban areas where the risk of development can be offset somewhat by lower overall costs or where the high cost of development can be reduced if the land does not need to be purchased. Arlington County, Virginia, has been especially successful in using this technique.[9]

Moreover, I recommend that public sector agencies lease publicly owned land instead of selling it, especially where leasing facilitates nonresidential development. In twenty to fifty years, most nonresidential development becomes ripe for conversion to a higher and better use, and hence higher lease payments go back to the public sector when leased property is redeveloped. In addition, the public sector can have more control over the timing and development features of private real estate investment when its land essentially makes it a partner in development. Even if lease payments are meager in the near term, in the long term retained public lands leased for private real estate development become an endowment benefiting public sector agencies.

*Air rights leases (ARLs).* Public sector agencies also own air rights that, on occasion, can be leveraged to stimulate private real estate investment. Most property rights include ownership of the land from the surface to the center of the earth and into the sky. In urban areas, air rights are used to construct buildings over both publicly and privately owned land. Air rights can also be transferred through a transfer of development right policy. For instance, if a parcel of land can accommodate a fifty-floor building but only a thirty-floor building is constructed, the owner may sell the remaining twenty floors to another developer for use elsewhere providing it is consistent with local development policies. Like land leases, the public sector may leverage private real estate development through the lease of air rights.

Revenues from land and air rights leases can be handled in several different ways in the workbook, including creating new fields to allow for them. A simple solution might be to include them as part of the cash throw-off option. This allows calculation of the public sector rate of return when public assets are partnered with private real estate interests.

*Share of net sales price (Sale).* The PDA may also seek a share of the net proceeds from the sale of a property. This can be triggered either at the actual sale of the property, at its refinancing with a commercial lender, or at a certain time in the future when the net sales price would be calculated and a payment made even if the owner held the project.

In the apartment example, all of the local leveraging tools noted in table 4.6 were used. Suppose also that, of the $500,000 in grants and fee waivers used, the PDA wants to recover $75,000. In addition, the PDA wants $2,000 per year in cash throw-off and 7.5 percent of the net sales proceeds after ten years. Whether the project sells after ten years is immaterial because the PDA wants to negotiate this revenue stream over a ten-year period, after which it is assumed the project has sufficient resources to be successful. Of course, it also receives interest from its own low-interest mezzanine loan to the development—in this case, 3 percent paid on a thirty-year mortgage amortization schedule.

Finally, like private investors, the PDA has its own IRR target. However, since its investment objectives are very different—it wants to stimulate development on this site and thereby stimulate economic activity elsewhere in the area—and it is exempt from federal, state, and local taxes, the return it needs may be quite low. Suppose the local PDA has a 5 percent IRR target. It may need this rate of return to help cover staff, overhead, and related expenses. Indeed, without some return on its investment, it might not have the funds needed to continue operating.

Table 4.7 shows the return for both the private investors and the PDA. Here we see that the private investors meet their cash-on-cash and leveraged return, and nearly the unleveraged target. While this solution meets nearly all financial objectives, it likely comes only after multiple iterations of analysis scenarios by both public and private partners to arrive at a solution acceptable to all parties.

**Table 4.7.**
Effect of the Use of Local Government Leveraging Tools on Investment Performance for
Private Investors and the PDA

| Performance Indicator | Target IRR | IRR before Leveraging | IRR after Leveraging | NPV before Leveraging | NPV after Leveraging |
|---|---|---|---|---|---|
| Cash-on-Cash after Year 3 | 10.00% | 5.24% | 10.00% | | |
| IRR—Unleveraged | 12.00% | 8.64% | 11.39% | ($1,744,152) | ($366,102) |
| IRR—Leveraged before tax | 25.00% | 11.52% | 32.80% | ($1,769,896) | $481,890 |
| RDA IRR | 5.00% | na | 5.67% | na | $89,619 |

# Public Financing of Parking Structures as a Form of Patient Equity

There is another application of patient capital that is crucial to the success of many redevelopment projects: financing parking structures.

Earlier in this book, I made the strong case that most of America's new development can occur on land that is currently parking lots and can include the redevelopment of structures that are on them. But parking structures will be needed to make many higher-density/intensity redevelopment projects work. No one firm, however, can shoulder the entire cost of a parking structure, and while several firms can collectively, it may be awkward managerially to do so. Moreover, when serving multiple projects in the same area, parking structures can generate important public benefits, such as more jobs, higher income, more development nearby, and more tax and fee revenue. I touched on the benefits of parking structures in the Shirlington case study in the introduction. Here, I explore how they can be financed.

Parking structures are expensive, running $25,000 to $40,000 per stall. Yet, without them, higher-density/intensity redevelopment is not possible. Possible sources of financing parking structures include the following:

*Parking revenue bonds (PRBs).* For a PRB, a public entity such as a PDA borrows money to build a structure and retires the debt through property tax assessments benefiting property in a defined area. Because the revenue bonds are often doubly tax-exempt, meaning bond holders receive interest payments free from federal and state taxes, and can extend twenty or more years, the annual tax assessment can be small.

*Tax increment financing (TIF)*. See the detailed review of TIF earlier in this chapter.

*Transient occupancy tax (TOT)*. This is a special tax assessed on hotels, motels, and even retail sales occurring in a benefit district that is used to retire parking bond debt as well as to help finance operations and maintenance.

*Parking fees (PFs)*. These come from hourly and monthly parking fees charged to shoppers, hotel guests, and employees working in the area, among others.

Public-private partnerships often use a combination of several of these techniques. Martindill (2012) outlines a common approach in which a P3 agreement engages in lease leaseback. The public partner enters into a ground lease with a private partner, who then builds the parking structure. The ground lease from the public partner to the private one can extend up to thirty years, but the parking structure leaseback from the private partner to the public one can be up to forty years. The public partner pays rent on the structure to the private partner (from a mix of sources that may include parking revenue bond payments, transient occupancy tax revenues, and parking fees) so that by the time the ground lease is due the parking structure debt has been retired. The parking structure reverts back to the public entity for a fee as low as one dollar.

The Excel workbook includes a special tab for estimating the investment returns from public provision of structured parking. The public sector does not need the kind of return the private sector needs both because its proceeds are tax free and, more importantly, because the form of public investment often leverages multiples of new development and associated tax and fee revenues that are not reported in the parking structure pro forma.

I conclude this chapter with some advice from a real estate investment mentor given to me many years ago:

*Protect against the downside because the upside will take care of itself.*

This does not mean avoiding risks, nor does it mean sticking with high rate of return options. It simply means being careful not to spend more than is necessary, accepting reasonable risks by not being too greedy and demanding short-term gains that are often unsustainable, and using financial tools that minimize vulnerability to both losses and opportunity costs.

## Conclusion

# America's Progress Depends on Redevelopment through Public-Private Partnerships

The twentieth century ushered in sprawling low-density development composed mostly of one land-use form—the single-family detached home—meeting market demands of a different era. That was then; this is now. The twenty-first century will be dominated by redevelopment. There are two reasons for this. First, this is where the market is headed, and, second, it is where the highest returns can be found. This does not mean downtowns will attract large shares of new development—they will not. The emerging American landscape will be dominated by infill and redevelopment of vast stretches of underdeveloped commercial corridors and suburban centers, especially those connected by transit. There will also be small-scale projects occurring, at an almost imperceptible rate, until a few decades later, entire metropolitan regions will have been transformed. A new generation of redevelopment-savvy planners and economic development officials needs to join forces with private sector interests to facilitate the desire of emerging markets to pursue redevelopment opportunities.

The broad public may not be aware of where we are in the continuum of development. Public officials and the people they serve assume that the future will be the past. The past—from 1946 to 2010—was dominated by shaping a landscape serving the baby boom. Between 1946 and 1964, the baby boom added 76 million children to the United States, representing an astonishing 40 percent of the nation's population by 1964. To the 1980s, parents of the boomers raised their children in suburbs composed mostly of single-family detached homes.

Boomers then raised their children in landscapes they knew and trusted. From the 1980s through the 2000s, boomers dominated America's housing market as millions were motivated to own large homes on large lots to raise growing families. During this period, Americans also enjoyed the highest household income in the nation's history. The numbers speak for themselves. Between 1989 and 2009 (Nelson 2013a): (1) boomer households accounted for 77 percent of the total change in housing demand; (2) of the 25 million new residential units built, 21 million, or about 80 percent, were detached; (3) the median size of a new home increased more during this period than during any other; and (4) more than 40 percent of all new detached homes were built on lots of more than one-half acre.

The needs of boomer households were met mostly by suburban communities whose land-use policies were greased by the "growth machine" in which development interests controlled local politics (Logan and Molotch 1987). As boomers moved into new suburbs, they became NIMBY (not-in-my-backyard) proponents, who opposed land-use changes generally and especially those changes that increased the supply of smaller or lower-value homes in the area. They did so even if advised that their home values might increase, largely because they did not trust claims of developers or assurances of local officials. The reason, as William Fischel (2001) astutely noted in *The Homevoter Hypothesis*, is because homeowners will protect their most valuable tangible asset—the home—against any threat that may reduce their home value, real or imagined. Fischel's theory explains much about behavior (see also Dehring, Depken, and Ward 2008). Détente between development interests and boomers was achieved through exclusionary zoning practices that distorted markets by pushing new development farther out, even when market signals showed growing demand for different neighborhood and community features.

We need to get out of the baby boom time warp. Land-use plans, subdivision and development codes, public infrastructure investments, tax policies, and mortgage financing created a built landscape that is no longer favored by emerging markets. This change is being led by the boomers themselves as they are empty-nesting, downsizing, and moving on. Ironically, it is the very exclusionary zoning policies and NIMBY-ism that thwarted housing choices that push boomers out of the communities they helped create. Boomers and the younger generations will combine forces to create America's next housing boom, but this time comprising smaller homes on smaller lots with improved accessibility to jobs, services, and shopping. Locations accessible to such public transit options as bus rapid transit, streetcars, and light rail will be especially favored. Indeed, to meet this emerging demand, every new residential unit built to 2040 would need to be within one-half mile of transit stations—and the demand would still not be met (Nelson 2013a). Unlike the mismatch with respect to mixed-use communities, meeting the market demand for transit accessibility can be accomplished by both accommodating new development where transit exists and extending transit to areas where it does not. This can be accomplished through redevelopment, especially of suburban commercial corridors and centers.

Markets will respond if these emerging trends can be facilitated by redevelopment along commercial corridors and in suburban centers, especially when they are connected by such surface transit options as bus rapid transit, streetcar, and light rail. Studies show that office, health care, cultural, convention/lodging, and service jobs are especially attracted to areas within one-quarter mile of transit stations (Guerra, Cervero, and Tischler 2011; Nelson et al. 2013). More interesting is that multifamily/attached owner and renter housing is attracted to areas within 1.25 miles of these facilities (Petheram et al. 2013). In looking strictly at capitalization rates, Pivo and Fisher (2010) found that properties near transit stations along suburban commercial corridors had 12.7 percent higher net incomes, 16.2 percent higher market values, 1.1 percent higher annual appreciation, and 0.9 percent higher annual total returns than other suburban office properties.

But redevelopment is not easy, nor is it something that can be done quickly. The Urban Land Institute, long a leader in advancing public-private partnerships, has identified these emerging themes that will refine P3 engagements in the future:[1]

- Continuing resource constraints on local governments will be the driving force in shaping new public-private partnerships.
- The P3 process needs to become more transparent so that all partners and key players easily understand what is being provided and by whom, and what the benefits are.
- To regain public trust and overcome community skepticism, the public and private sectors must answer questions about and provide

supporting information to ensure maximum financial scrutiny.

- Improvement in the use of standardized metrics to assess proposals and agreements is needed to ensure transparency as well as to stream-line P3 processes and outcomes.
- The public sector needs to make the entitlement process more efficient and predictable to reduce some of the private sector risks.
- In its role as civic leaders, the private sector should reassume the lead in setting the vision for large areas of a community, if not the entire community. It has the resources and capacity to assume this role at a time when public resources are limited. Indeed, this has been a key role of the private sector in urban development historically.

Though the market exists, as do the overall economic benefits, the barri-ers confronting redevelopment are daunting. But overcoming them to achieve optimal redevelopment can lead to higher employment, higher wages, more homeowners, fewer foreclosures, enhanced fiscal resources to advance qual-ity of life, improved environmental quality, and better overall public health. Quoting the Urban Land Institute: "Now is the time to accelerate the use of public-private partnerships to manage the complexities of redevelopment ef-ficiently and successfully" (Corrigan et al. 2005, 42). Because the future of the United States is redevelopment, the future of redevelopment is effective public-private partnerships. Without them, the United States cannot move forward.

# Appendix A: Workbook User Guide

*Foundations of Real Estate Finance for Development: A Guide for Public-Private Partnerships* includes a Microsoft Excel workbook for instructional purposes only (http://islandpress.org/ReshapeMetroAmerica). No warranties are offered or implied for any purpose. Further, there is no warranty as to errors or omissions. It is assumed that the analyst is competent with Excel.

The workbook includes real estate finance instructional tabs for these development types:

Residential for sale
Residential rental
Office
Retail
Hotel
Industrial
Parking
Mixed-use summary (as combinations of different development
    types)

The front page of the workbook includes a Quick Start Guide (http://ReshapeMetroAmerica.org).

A few quick and easy steps will get you started at modeling prototype buildings and testing land-use regulations.

**1. Save this workbook as a file with a new name to preserve it as a master.**

Be sure to save as a separate file each analysis that you wish to archive.

**2. Decide what kind of development you want to analyze.**

If you are analyzing a single use, go to the proper tab (Res. Owner, Res. Rental, Office, Retail, or Accommodation)

If you are analyzing a mixed-use development, use all of the desirable land-use tabs (Res. Owner, Res. Rental, Office, Retail, or Accommodation) *You must enter input fields only in uses that are being analyzed.*

The mixed-use tab will provide the analysis summary.

**3. Only input figures into cells that are Red-Bold.**

The structure of all of the tabs is similar. I will walk through the Residential Rental tab to describe each step, focusing on analyst inputs. I will describe the inputs and results for the solution reported in chapter 4, tables 4.6 and 4.7. The workbook for real estate finance is limited to before-tax cash flow and net sales proceeds before tax. Tax implications to individuals, corporations, trusts, or other entities are therefore not addressed.

# Organization of the Analyst Guide

The Analyst Guide has four parts:

A. Review of investment targets and performance
B. Project finances
C. Review of public partner tools
D. Annual operating statement and proceeds from sale

The User Guide refers to tables generally in the order in which they are shown in the worksheet. Moreover, for ease of reference, each of the headings below corresponds to table titles in the worksheet.

## A. Investment Targets and Performance

At the very top left of each worksheet is a summary of investment targets and performance. The analyst can quickly scroll to it to see how each change affects the performance targets, which are summarized here.

*Cash-on-Cash After Year 3* is the before tax cash flow divided by equity investment. The figure reported is based on Year 3, which is the assumed year of rent stabilization. The analyst can change this to an alternate year by changing the cell reference. In this example, the target of 10.00 percent is reached.

*Return on Project Cost (Unleveraged Return)* shows the target return compared to the actual internal rate of return (IRR) and net present value (NPV) for the project as a whole considering all project costs. In this case, the target 12.00 percent is not met, as the actual IRR is 11.39 percent and the NPV is –$366,102.

*Return on Investor Equity (Leveraged Return Before Tax)* shows the target return compared to the actual IRR (NPV for just the investors' equity). In this case, the target 25.00 percent is met, as the actual IRR is 32.80 percent and the NPV is $481,890.

*Debt Service Coverage Ratio (Year 3)* is the NOI divided by the sum of all debt service (DS). Lenders normally want to see at least a 1.25 ratio at the stabilization year (which the analyst can change mechanically). In this case, the debt service coverage ratio (DSCR) is below the target 1.25 but only because the low-interest mezzanine financing added to the senior debt pushes total DS above the target. Whether the DSCR for all DS should meet the target is a decision to be made by mezzanine lenders.

*Return on Public Participation* is conceptually the same as Return on Investor Equity except the "equity" is the public partner investments, such as low interest loans, grants, and other inducements.

## B. Project Finances

This part reviews project costs, calculating net operating income, debt financing, and investor equity.

HOLDING PERIOD

In this line, the analyst will need to frame the period of analysis based on an increment of five years to thirty years. In this case, the Holding Period is ten years.

PROJECT DEVELOPMENT COSTS

The next set of inputs relates to Project Development Costs.

If the project already exists or is being purchased turnkey (which occurs when a developer transfers a newly finished product to a buyer), the analyst will report the price in the Project Purchase Price cell.

An alternative is to use the Detailed Development Costs section to separate major component parts of a new development project into Total Hard Costs, Soft Costs, and Land Cost. The analyst needs to input these figures. The hard and soft cost components may be used for tax credit and building write-down analysis. The soft cost component may be useful for fee waiver analysis. The land cost component may be useful for land write-down analysis.

There is the possibility that a zone change or other adjustment to land-use controls can increase the amount of development that can occur on the site. This possibility is discussed next. However, if it occurs, it will change development costs. The assumption is made that increasing development on the site will increase hard and soft costs proportionately, but not land costs. A 50 percent increase in residential units, for instance, will increase the total project cost by $3,937,500 to a total of $13,312,500, but the average price per unit will fall from $187,500 to $177,500. As an alternative, the analyst could simply report either the Project Purchase Price or the Detailed Development Costs for the project as a consequence of a change in allowable development.

PROJECT PARAMETERS

Here the analyst inputs basic project parameters.

The analyst starts with the assumed number of Initial Residential units planned—in this case, fifty. Any adjustment in the number of units, up or down, perhaps through changes in land-use controls, can be included in Alternative Residential Units. The number of units for analysis is the Alternative Residential Units if greater than 0; otherwise, it is Initial Residential units planned.

The analyst also includes the Land area acres, which is used internally to calculate the Units per acre. The Square Feet per unit is an average of the gross building area divided by all residential units, so it includes hallways, lobbies, elevators, and other common areas. The Total project size, square feet (Number of units for analysis multiplied by Square feet per unit) and Floor Area Ratio (FAR) [(Total built space) divided by (Land area in acres multiplied by 43,560 square feet per acre)] are internally calculated.

### NET OPERATING INCOME ASSUMPTIONS

In this table, the analyst inputs basic assumptions about Monthly Rent/Unit, Miscellaneous Income (% of GSI), Vacancy rate, Concessions, Bad Debt rate, and Annual Operating Costs/unit.

The Annual Operating Costs/unit includes Replacement Reserves (RR). The analyst can choose to include them or not. RR is a small amount of money set aside from each unit periodically to cover the cost of major capital repairs, such as roofs, heating/cooling/ventilation, exterior painting, and related. When the building is sold, the balance in the RR account goes to the seller and is thus counted as income at project sale (since it was deducted from income in prior years). If the holding period is short, perhaps ten years or less, the analyst may choose to ignore RR. If the holding period is longer, the analyst could include RR as an annual expense, assuming that, when the building is sold, all of the RR will have been expended by then (perhaps to update the building and therefore maximize its sale price potential).

### NET OPERATING INCOME ANALYSIS

At this stage, the analyst will have the information needed to calculate the net operating income (NOI). All of the figures are derived from assumptions made in earlier tables.

INITIAL PROJECT VALUE

From the ROI, the analyst can estimate the overall market value of the project along with other key indicators, as shown in the next table.

The Cap Rate (Yield to Costs) is internally calculated as NOI/Project Cost. The project's first year Before-Tax Cash Flow (BTCF) is calculated as NOI less Debt Service. The Return on Equity (Year 1) is the BTCF/Equity and is also internally calculated. The investor's equity stake in the project is discussed later.

To estimate current market value, however, the analyst needs to make an assumption on what is called Going in Cap Rate, or the market-based Cap Rate at the beginning of the project. In this case, perhaps the information comes from a commercial broker or lender or other professional source. At the 6.00 percent Cap Rate, the Project Market Value would be $9,445,883. The Net Project Value is the difference between Project Market Value and Project Cost. In this case, once started, the investment is worth slightly more than the cost, though not much.

ESCALATION

The next table has the analyst making assumptions about annual average escalation in PGI and Operating Expenses. There should be sound reasons for PGI escalation being higher than Operating Expenses escalation because if PGI is even a small percentage point higher the results can be very favorable to investors over time—sometimes too favorable. It is better to be conservative in escalation assumptions.

PROJECT SALE ASSUMPTIONS

Real estate investment analyses usually assume termination of the investment with a sale, which is the subject of the next table.

In this table, the analyst inputs the assumed Terminal Cap Rate and Sales Cost, both as percentages. Much as the Going in Cap Rate applied to the first-year ROI estimated current market value, so does the Terminal Cap Rate apply to the ROI in the year of sale. In this case, perhaps the analyst assumes a lower cap rate in the future (hence higher value) because nearby development will occur, lifting the values of all projects. In addition, this project may be favorably located in the path of infill and redevelopment and, combined with a growing market, may become an increasingly desirable place for future investment.

Second, the analyst inputs the assumed percent of sales costs in relation to the sale price. Usually, the higher the property value, the lower the sales cost as a percent of the sale price will be.

DEBT FINANCING

Senior Debt is the principal source of long-term financing. The analyst needs to input the loan-to-value (L/V) ratio. The Mortgage amount is internally calculated. The analyst can also override the calculation by inputting a number directly into the cell. The analyst then inputs the annual mortgage Rate and Amortization Period, Years. The loan payments will be noted later.

This is also done for Mezzanine Debt with one difference. The Loan Support amount is taken from the Loan Support part of the Public Partner Financing Tools block that will be presented below. The L/V ratio is internally calculated. The analyst again inputs the annual mortgage Rate and Amortization Period, Years. The loan payments will be noted later.

Many real estate investments borrow funds from multiple sources. If so, the analyst may need to edit the worksheet to add more loans by (1) increasing the Debt Financing table to account for them and (2) adding new Mortgage Amortization tables as needed at the bottom of the worksheet. The sum of all mortgage payments reported on the annual statements shown below will also need to be adjusted.

DEBT FINANCING AND EQUITY REQUIREMENTS

Once costs and debt financing are determined, the equity requirements become known. The Excel table summarizes debt and shows the extent to which public partner tools may offset development costs and thereby reduce equity.

## C. Public Partner Leveraging Tools

This part reviews the suite of tools public partners may have available to offset project costs or otherwise help with financing. It includes a review of how the public partner may itself be a financial partner in a public-private partnership.

### Public Partner Tools Summary

The first table in this part is an overall summary of categories of tools used to leverage private partner investment. Offsets to Project Cost include Tax Credits net to the project, Fee Reductions, and Grants. The categories will be discussed next.

### Tax Abatements and Reimbursements

This table allows the analyst to address four of the ways in which the local government may use sales and property tax tools to help with a project's cash flow, especially in the early years (see chapter 4).

The first one is property tax abatement, in which the analyst inputs the percent of the locally assessed property taxes, PTA (%), that may be abated for each year up to ten years. The analyst will also need to input the effective property tax rate as a percent that the local government will abate. The analyst can extend the abatement period by adding rows and also amending the operating expense statement accordingly. The abatement is shown as income in the Operating Expense Statement.

The second is the sales tax abatement percent, STA (%), which the local government is willing to abate relative to the sales taxes it would receive. This applies only to projects that generate sales taxes to the public partner. It is also shown as income in the Operating Expense Statement.

There will be occasions when some features of a development project that otherwise may have been borne by the development can be financed from tax increment financing. If TIF provides a onetime benefit concurrent with the project opening, it could be considered a grant (see below). But if property taxes pledged for TIF purposes pay for improvements over time that the developer would have paid anyway, in effect the developer's own property taxes are used for this purpose. The analyst would input the dollars of benefit accruing to the developer for each relevant year in the TIF ($) column.

Another, more common, variant is where the local government needs the developer to install improvements (such as road widening, traffic lights, and upgraded utilities) as part of the project construction cost. That cost could be reimbursed over time from the property taxes the developer would have paid to the local government, until such time as that cost is fully reimbursed. These are called infrastructure reimbursement agreements (IRAs). If this is applicable, the analyst will note the dollar amounts for the relevant years in the IRA ($) column.

PUBLIC PARTNER FINANCING TOOLS

A host of tools are available to public partners in P3 arrangements. I categorize them into Fee Reductions, Grants, Tax Credits, Loan Support, and Land and Air Leases. The details of each tool within each category are reviewed in chapter 4.

**Fee reductions** include an amount paid by a development for permitting, inspection, or other onetime purpose. Fee reductions reduce the soft costs of development and thereby the project cost incurred by the developer. The amount of equity required by investors is also reduced.

**Grants and Capital Investment Offsets** are funds paid from a source other than the developer to defray the cost of land (land write down), the structure (building write down), infrastructure, or other purpose or a combination of purposes. Like fee reductions, they reduce hard costs, soft costs, and/or land costs, thereby reducing the overall project cost incurred by the developer. This in turn can reduce investor equity requirements.

**Tax credits** are unique in that the owners of those credits can reduce the federal taxes they owe dollar for dollar up to a certain annual cap and can continue taking credits as needed over a prescribed number of years. The credit is effectively a grant against project costs. More importantly, it can greatly reduce the need for private equity investors. Often, in return for the credit, the property must be used for specific purposes, such as providing low-income housing at rents below the prevailing market. The public partner does not participate directly in providing the tax credits, but it can be instrumental in packing the proposal.

**Loan support** tools often provide below-market mezzanine financing in part because, as a nonprofit, the public partner's return is exempt from taxes and in part because the public partner may view the loan for one property as a stimulus to encourage other investments nearby. Between senior and mezzanine debt, equity requirements can be reduced. Because earnings from public partner mezzanine financing can be reinvested as interest is received, and as loans are retired, some versions of loan support are called revolving loan funds.

**Land and air rights leases** can be used in situations where the public partner owns real estate that it wishes to keep but is willing to lease its rights to the private partner, typically for fifty to ninety-nine years, which may be renewed. Mechanically, the analyst zeroes out land costs, but the lease amount is added to the Land/Air Rights Lease payment of the public participation section, which is discussed next.

PUBLIC PARTNER PARTICIPATION

The last section addresses the return to the public partner role, which is discussed in detail in chapter 4. I recommend that, whenever a public entity contributes money (as opposed to making changes in land-use controls) to a private investment, it considers earning a return on it. Forms of return can include Capital Recovery (from grants), Annual Cash Throw-Off, Annual Land/Air Lease, and a Share of Net Sales Proceeds, all of which are described in chapter 4. The public partner should also establish the Target Return over the holding period.

### D. Annual Operating Statement and Proceeds from Sale

This final part addresses the annual net revenues from operations and proceeds for sale after the holding period. The analyst does nothing because outputs are automaticall calculated from the analyst's inputs. Five tables are generated.

## Annual Operating Statement

Key information from the Annual Operating Statement includes Potential Gross Income (PGI), Effective Gross Income (EGI), Net Operating Income (NOI), Debt Service, and Before-Tax Cash Flow. These outputs become the inputs to other internally generated tables to report market value of the project in future years, sale price, and overall return.

Notice in this example that cash-on-cash rises dramatically. This is because, as income increases by the assumed escalation rate, the equity contribution is fixed in time, at the beginning of the project. Some analysts will impute the value of equity contributions over time by at least the escalation rate if not the rate of a reasonably secure alternative investment, such as high-quality taxable corporate bonds. The cash-on-cash return based on the "opportunity cost" of an alternative investment for the equity would be much less. The analyst could modify the workbook to allow for this.

## Proceeds from Sale

The next table internally calculates the net proceeds from sale.

For the end of the holding period—ten years in this example—it internally calculates the Gross Sales Price based on (NOI/Terminal Cap Rate). The Net Sales price is further adjusted by the assumed cost of sale. The Net Sales price Less Mortgage Balance generates the Net Sales Proceeds.

## Return—Unleveraged (Project Cost)

The next table internally calculates the return from the unleveraged project cost.

The total project investment after adjustments to the project cost is shown as a negative number in Year 0. In the sale year, Year 10, the Net Sales Price is reported. For each year, from Year 1 through Year 10, the NOI is also reported. The IRR-Project Cost and the NPV-Project Cost consider the annual NOI plus Net Sales Proceeds relative to the Net Project Cost. In this analysis, the target returns are not quite met.

RETURN—LEVERAGED (BEFORE TAX)

There are two differences between the previous version and this one. Instead of NOI, Before-Tax Cash Flow is included; it is NOI less debt service. The Before-Tax Cash Flow plus Net Sales Proceeds is compared to Equity, instead of to Net Project Cost. In this example, both the IRR and the NPV targets are exceeded.

RETURN—PUBLIC PARTNER PARTICIPATION

The public partner contributions on which it bases its target return in this case consist of the low-interest Loan and the Capital Recovery (from grants) for a Total Public Participation of $1,675,000. Annual cash flow comes from Mezzanine Debt Service, Cash Throw-Off, and Air/Land Lease Payments. The Sale Proceeds are based on the Share of Net Sales Proceeds as per a development agreement between the public and private partners—in this case, 7.5 percent. It shows that the public partner participation return targets are met.

The bottom line return figures from these last three tables are reported at the very top of the worksheet so the analyst knows quickly what the overall results are.

The rest of the worksheet consists of mortgage amortization tables for the senior and mezzanine debt, and summed for both.

# Appendix B: Simplified Depreciation Periods for Land Uses

| Type | Use | Life |
|---|---|---|
| Industrial | Associated Industrial | 60 |
| Industrial | Condo Industrial | 50 |
| Industrial | Flex | 50 |
| Industrial | Ind—Light—Mfg | 60 |
| Industrial | Ind Common Master | 50 |
| Industrial | Ind Heavy Mfg | 60 |
| Industrial | Ind Light Shell | 50 |
| Industrial | Industrial Mixed | 50 |
| Industrial | Industrial/Other | 50 |
| Industrial | Ind. Conversion | 50 |
| Industrial | Other Improvements | 60 |
| Institutional | Church | 60 |
| Institutional | Golf Course | 35 |
| Institutional | Gov Bldg/Land | 45 |
| Institutional | Hospital | 50 |
| Institutional | Nursing Hospital | 50 |
| Institutional | Other Exempt | 45 |
| Institutional | Post Office | 60 |
| Institutional | Public | 45 |
| Institutional | School | 45 |
| Institutional | School Private | 45 |

| | | |
|---|---|---|
| Mixed Use | Comm Imps in Res Zone | 60 |
| Mixed Use | Conversion Other | 45 |
| Mixed Use | Office Conversion | 60 |
| Mixed Use | Office Mixed | 45 |
| Mixed Use | Retail Conversion | 55 |
| Mixed Use | Retail Mixed | 50 |
| Office | Associated Office | 60 |
| Office | Condo Office | 60 |
| Office | Ind—RE | 60 |
| Office | Medical Office | 50 |
| Office | Office | 60 |
| Office | Office Comm Master | 60 |
| Office | Parking Structure | 45 |
| Retail | Associated Retail | 55 |
| Retail | Auto Dealership | 50 |
| Retail | Auto Showroom | 50 |
| Retail | Car Wash | 30 |
| Retail | Comm-Parkg Lot | 45 |
| Retail | Commercial/Other | 45 |
| Retail | Community Mall | 50 |
| Retail | Condo Retail | 55 |
| Retail | Convenience Store | 45 |
| Retail | Department Store | 55 |
| Retail | Discount Store | 40 |
| Retail | Discount Warehouse | 40 |
| Retail | Drug Store | 45 |
| Retail | Fast Food Restaurant | 40 |
| Retail | Lounge | 45 |
| Retail | Market | 45 |
| Retail | Regional Mall | 55 |
| Retail | Restaurant | 45 |
| Retail | Retail Comm Master | 55 |
| Retail | Retail Service | 55 |
| Retail | Retail Store | 55 |
| Retail | Strip Center | 45 |

| | | |
|---|---|---|
| Retail | Used Car Lot | 40 |
| Service and Entertainment | Apt High Rise | 60 |
| Service and Entertainment | Auto Service Center | 45 |
| Service and Entertainment | Bank | 60 |
| Service and Entertainment | Bed and Breakfast | 65 |
| Service and Entertainment | Bowling Alley | 40 |
| Service and Entertainment | Comm Condo Park Stal | 0 |
| Service and Entertainment | Comm Condo Storg Unt | 50 |
| Service and Entertainment | Condo Hotel | 50 |
| Service and Entertainment | Day Care Center | 45 |
| Service and Entertainment | Fraternal Building | 55 |
| Service and Entertainment | Group Care Home | 55 |
| Service and Entertainment | Health Club | 50 |
| Service and Entertainment | Hotel | 60 |
| Service and Entertainment | Hotel—Limited | 60 |
| Service and Entertainment | Hotel Comm Master | 50 |
| Service and Entertainment | Laundromat | 35 |
| Service and Entertainment | Mini Lube | 40 |
| Service and Entertainment | Mortuary | 50 |
| Service and Entertainment | Motel | 45 |
| Service and Entertainment | Neighborhood Ctr | 45 |
| Service and Entertainment | Reception Center | 55 |
| Service and Entertainment | Service Garage | 40 |
| Service and Entertainment | Service Station | 25 |
| Service and Entertainment | Theater | 50 |
| Warehouse and Storage | Airport—Exempt | 30 |
| Warehouse and Storage | Airport Hangar | 30 |
| Warehouse and Storage | Cold Storage | 50 |
| Warehouse and Storage | Distribution Whse | 55 |
| Warehouse and Storage | Exempt Concessnaire | 30 |
| Warehouse and Storage | Exempt Hangar—Vac | 30 |
| Warehouse and Storage | Loft | 60 |
| Warehouse and Storage | Mini Warehouse | 45 |
| Warehouse and Storage | Office/Warehouse | 60 |
| Warehouse and Storage | Storage Garage | 45 |

| | | |
|---|---|---|
| Warehouse and Storage | Storage Warehouse | 55 |
| Warehouse and Storage | Transit Warehouse | 45 |
| Residential | Residential | 150 |

*Source*: Adapted from Marshall & Swift (2014). Marshall Valuation Service. Los Angeles, CA: Marshall & Swift.

# Notes

PREFACE

1   It is as though American politicians and policy-makers, and the public who put them into office, learned little from the savings-and-loan debacle. History did repeat itself in this context.

2   When considering the cost of living, home values in large parts of the nation may not reach their highs of the 2000s for many decades if ever.

INTRODUCTION

1   See "Public-Private Partnerships Terms Related to Building and Facility Partnerships," http://www.gao.gov/special.pubs/Gg99071.pdf (accessed December 9, 2013).

2   Real estate developers are popularly considered to be very successful with their projects and income. In the same breath, it seems that they are often lionized and reviled. As with many other popular perceptions, reality is very different. Highly successful developers are about as rare as highly successful architects, attorneys, and actors. While some developers certainly make millions annually (though the successful ones reinvest profits into new ventures), a much larger number of highly experienced professionals in the industry earn an average of about $200,000 annually (see http://www1.salary.com/ Top-Real-Estate-Executive-Salary.html).

CHAPTER 1

1   In our book, we used the term *public goods*, although in the context of planning and development, this usually relates to maximizing environmental quality.

2   Water and wastewater facilities are provided by a separate special district.

3   For details, see the history and redevelopment details at http://www.arlington virginiausa.com/development/major-projects/development-shirlington/.

4 Formally, the test for the null hypothesis where there is no statistically significant effect of compactness on outcomes, all things considered. Using ordinary least squares regression, the double-log regression coefficients are interpreted as an X-percent change in an independent variable, such as employment change, that is associated with a Y-percent change in the compactness index, the dependent variable.

5 See "City of Winnipeg Quality of Life Indicators," http://www.iisd.org/pdf/wpg.qoli.pdf (accessed December 7, 2013).

6 For all equations, the controlling variables are the natural logs of population 2000, ratio of population 2005 to 2000 (a measure of growth), median household income in 2000 dollars, share of manufacturing jobs to all jobs in 2000, and share of government jobs to all jobs in 2000 plus binary variables for eight of the nine census divisions (excluding the West North Central as the referent) for regional controls. The dependent variable for the Ewing Compactness Index score is also logged. For brevity in the text, I only report the elasticity coefficient for selected economic outcome variables along with the equation $R^2$ and the $t$-score derived probability level, $p$, both in parentheses.

7 Estimated from http://en.wikipedia.org/wiki/Timeline_of_the_United_States_housing_bubble.

8 I am indebted to work done by Parsons Brinkerhoff for the Utah Transit Authority for identifying these barriers, which I adapt here. As members of a peer review committee working with both groups, we drafted a handbook for the UTA that will help guide infill and redevelopment around transit stations and elsewhere.

9 I am indebted to Fregonese Associates for this case study.

10 Northam (1971) and Bowman and Pagano (2004) addressed mostly vacant land, whereas I extend the concepts to all urban land whether vacant or developed.

11 The "floor" might be indexed for the cost of inflation or some other adjustment and might sunset after a certain number of years.

12 In some states, the act of zoning property vests it so that, if rezoning is done concurrent with plan adoption, there is little incentive by the property owner to sell at a reasonable price.

13 When visiting Germany some years ago, I interviewed local planning directors who faced the same concerns about property owners having excessive expectations of their property value. The approach used in many German communities and regions is to allocate development rights to target parcels that if exercised would meet market needs identified through the planning process, but if not exercised within five years, those rights would expire and then be reallocated to other property. This allows landowners to sell or hold their land as they wish but removes long-term speculative expectations, thus providing developers with a reasonable supply of willing sellers at reasonably competitive prices.

14 My estimate.

15 I am paraphrasing the program description (see Atlanta Development Authority ca. 2013).

16 See http://www.atlantaemergingmarkets.com/IncentiveToolkit/IncentiveToolkit. html.

## CHAPTER 2

1 With permission.

2 Kansas Statutes Annotated, § 12-1770a(c).

3 See http://www.hillsboro2020.org/FileLib/H2020ActionPlan2010_Web.pdf.

4 These figures are based on the Commercial Buildings Energy Consumption Survey for 2003, http://www.eia.gov/consumption/commercial/data/archive/cbecs/cbecs2003/detailed_tables_2003/2003setl/2003pdf/b1.pdf (accessed November 24, 2013).

5 I am grateful to Alex Joyce of Fregonese Associates for assistance in preparing this case study.

6 See http://www.marshallswift.com/.

7 This summary is adapted from the American Association of State Highway and Transportation Officials from http://www.transportation-finance.org/pdf/funding_financing/legislation_regulations/state_local_legislation/DEVELOPMENT_AGREEMENT_ACT.pdf.

8 See Julian Conrad Juergensmeyer and Thomas E. Roberts (2013) for an extensive review of such powers in regulating development and redevelopment.

## CHAPTER 3

1 See http://www.realtor.org/ncommsrc.nsf/files/commercial%20real%20estate%20glossary.pdf/$file/commercial%20real%20estate%20glossary.pdf.

2 Pro forma is Latin for "as a matter of form." Real estate pro formas include most of the elements I present in this chapter plus often many others. See Peiser and Hamilton (2012) for elaborations.

3 These are not to be confused with an East Coast city garden apartment, which means the basement floor of a building or a row house.

4 I am indebted to Joe Molinaro of the National Association of Realtors for many of the insights contained in the retail subsection.

5 The real estate literature and industry are not consistent in some of their terminology, but the concepts are the same.

6 Much of this discussion is adapted from http://blog.realtyshares.com/post/43352590840/the-real-estate-capital-stack.

7 Christopher B. Leinberger discusses the nineteen standard real estate investment

types, most of which have very short useful lives and need to be repurposed, if not replaced, within twenty to forty years. See his article "The 19 Building Types That Caused the Recession" at http://www.theatlanticcities.com/jobs-and-economy/2011/10/buildings-that-caused-recession/345/.

8　With apologies to Donald Rumsfeld, who, while serving as US Secretary of Defense, stated in the context of the Iraq invasion of 2002: "There are known knowns; there are things we know that we know. There are known unknowns; that is to say, there are things that we now know we don't know. But there are also unknown unknowns—there are things we do not know we don't know." See http://www.defense.gov/transcripts/transcript.aspx?transcriptid=2636.

9　See James R. DeLisle, *A Primer on Discounted Cash Flow Analysis*, available at http://jrdelisle.com/cases_tutorials/FinPrimTuts/jPrimer_DCFv27.pdf.

## CHAPTER 4

1　The Environmental Protection Agency in *Infrastructure Financing Options for Transit-Oriented Development* (2013) has these categories of financing: (1) reduction in direct fees, including user and utility fees and congestion pricing; (2) debt tools, including private debt, bond financing, and federal and state infrastructure debt mechanisms; (3) credit assistance, such as federal and state credit assistance tools and the Transportation Infrastructure Finance and Innovation Act (TIFIA); (4) equity contributions through public-private partnerships and infrastructure investment funds; (5) publicly provided value capture, such as waivers and/or reductions of developer fees and exactions as well as funds from special districts, tax increment financing, and joint development; (6) grants and other philanthropic sources ranging from federal transportation and community and economic development grants to foundation grants and investments to local nonprofit sources; and (7) emerging tools, such as structured funds, land banks, and infrastructure banks. See http://www.epa.gov/smartgrowth/pdf/2013-0122-TOD-infrastructure-financing-report.pdf.

2　See http://www.epa.gov/brownfields/glossary.htm.

3　Much of this discussion is adapted from the Wisconsin Department of Revenue, http://www.revenue.wi.gov/pubs/slf/tif/cvmanual.html (accessed January 2, 2013).

4　They go by other names in several states but conceptually they are all the same.

5　A state-by-state review of programs and recipients is provided by the *New York Times*: http://www.nytimes.com/interactive/2012/12/01/us/government-incentives.html#AL.

6　Much of this discussion is based on information provided by HUD at http://www.huduser.org/portal/datasets/lihtc.html (accessed January 3, 2013).

7　If tax-exempt bonds are also used to build the project, the maximum credit is 40 percent of the structure cost or 4 percent annually for ten years.

8 The actual process of syndication and who is eligible to participate is complex. See http://www.occ.gov/topics/community-affairs/resource-directories/tax-credits/tax-credits-lihtc.html.

9 I especially recommend the Shirlington, Virginia, development project reviewed at http://www.arlingtonvirginiausa.com/development/major-projects/development-shirlington/.

## CONCLUSION

1 This list is adapted from the Urban Land Institute's web page "Innovative Public/Private Partnerships and Finance," http://www.uli.org/research/centers-initiatives/center-for-capital-markets/capital-markets-forums-education-events/charles-h-shaw-forum-innovative-public-private-partnerships/ (accessed January 21, 2014).

# References

Barr, Michael S. 2005. "Credit Where It Counts: The Community Reinvestment Act and Its Critics." *New York University Law Review* 80:513–652.

Blais, Pamela. 2010. *Perverse Cities: Hidden Subsidies, Wonky Policy and Urban Sprawl*. Vancouver: University of British Columbia.

Bourne, Larry S. 1967. *Private Redevelopment of the Central City*. Toronto: University of Toronto.

Bowman, Ann O'M., and Michael A. Pagano. 2004. *Terra Incognita: Vacant Land and Urban Strategies*. Washington, DC: Georgetown University Press.

Callies, David L., and Julie A. Tappendorf. 2014. *Development by Agreement: Tool Kit for Land Developers and Local Governments*. Chicago: American Bar Association.

Ciccone, Antonio, and Robert E. Hall. 1996. "Productivity and the Density of Economic Activity." *American Economic Review* 86 (1): 54–70.

City of Hillsboro, Oregon. 2010. *Downtown Hillsboro Urban Renewal Plan*. Hillsboro, OR: City of Hillsboro Planning Department. Accessed January 4, 2013, at http://www.downtowndevelopment.com/pdf/Hills_Dntn%20Hillsboro%20 UR%20PLAN%20FINAL_052010.pdf.

Colean, Miles L. 1953. *Renewing Our Cities*. New York: Twentieth Century Fund.

Corrigan, Mary Beth, Jack Hambene, William Hudnut III, Rachelle L. Levitt, John Stainback, Richard Ward, and Nicole Witenstein. 2005. *Ten Principles for Successful Public/Private Partnerships*. Washington, DC: Urban Land Institute.

Dehring, C., C. Depken, II, and M. Ward. 2008. "A Direct Test of the Homevoter Hypothesis." *Journal of Urban Economics* 64 (1): 155–70. http://dx.doi.org/10.1016/j. jue.2007.11.001.

Department of the Treasury. 2012. *A New Economic Analysis of Infrastructure Investment*. Washington, DC: U.S. Department of the Treasury. Accessed December 13, 2013 from http://www.treasury.gov/resource-center/economic-policy/docu ments/20120323infrastructurereport.pdf.

Duncan and Associates. 2012. *Impact Fee Land Use Assumptions and Capital Improvements Plan, 2012–2022*. Albuquerque, NM: City of Albuquerque.

Dunham-Jones, Ellen, and June Williamson. 2011. *Retrofitting Suburbia: Urban Design Solutions for Redesigning Suburbs*. 2nd ed. New York: Wiley.

Ewing, Reid, Keith Bartholomew, Steve Winkelman, Jerry Walters, and Don Chen. 2008. *Growing Cooler: The Evidence on Urban Development and Climate Change*. Washington, DC: Urban Land Institute.

Ewing, Reid, and Shima Hamidi. 2014. *Measuring Sprawl 2014*. Washington, DC: Smart Growth America.

Fischel, William. 2001. *The Homevoter Hypothesis: How Home Values Influence Local Government*. Cambridge, MA: Harvard University Press.

Graaskamp, James A. 1981. *Fundamentals of Real Estate Development*. Washington, DC: Urban Land Institute.

Greenstein, Rosalind, and Yesim Sungu-Eryilmaz. 2004. *Recycling the City: The Use and Reuse of Urban Land*. Cambridge, MA: Lincoln Institute of Land Policy.

Guerra, Erick, Robert Cervero, and Daniel Tischler. 2011. *The Half-Mile Circle: Does It Best Represent Transit Station Catchments?* Berkeley: University of California Transportation Center.

Holzheimer, Terry. 2008. "Creating an Improved Urban Village: The Redevelopment of Shirlington, Virginia." Accessed November 24, 2013, at https://www.planning.org/eda/spotlight/2008/win.htm.

Institute of Transportation Engineers. 2012. *Trip Generation Manual*. 9th ed. Washington, DC: Institute of Transportation Engineers.

Juergensmeyer, Julian Conrad, and Thomas Roberts. 2013. *Land Use Planning and Development Regulation Law*. 3rd ed. Minneapolis: West Publishing.

Kohlhepp, Daniel B. 2012. *The Real Estate Development Matrix*. Baltimore: Johns Hopkins Carey Business School.

Leinberger, Christopher B. 2001. *Financing Progressive Development*. Capital Xchange (web-based publication of the Brookings Institution and Harvard University, available at http://www.brookings.edu/research/articles/2001/05/metropolitan policy-leinberger).

———. 2007. *Back to the Future: The Need for Patient Equity in Real Estate Development Finance*. Washington, DC: The Brookings Institution.

———. 2008. *Option of Urbanism*. Washington, DC: Island Press.

Logan, Gregg, Stephanie Siejka, and Shyam Kannan. 2007. *The Market for Smart Growth*. Bethesda, MD: Robert Charles Lesser Company (RCLCO).

Logan, John R., and Harvey Molotch. 1987. *Urban Fortunes: The Political Economy of Place*. Berkeley: University of California Press.

Martindill, Martin D. 2012. "P3 as an Alternate Approach to Financing Parking Structures." International Parking Institute (June), 30–32, accessed December 19,

2013, at http://www.timhaahs.com/articles/12-06_Getting_Your_Ps_in_a_Row_-_ Martindill.pdf.

McCann, Barbara A., and Reid Ewing. 2003. *Measuring the Health Effects of Sprawl: A National Analysis of Physical Activity, Obesity and Chronic Disease.* Washington, DC: Smart Growth America.

Mertens, Jean-François, and Anna Rubinchik. 2006. *Intergenerational Equity and the Discount Rate for Cost-Benefit Analysis.* CORE Discussion Papers 2006091. Louvain, Belgium: Université catholique de Louvain, Center for Operations Research and Econometrics (CORE). http://dx.doi.org/10.2139/ssrn.949714.

Miles, Mike E., Gayle L. Berens, Mark J. Eppli, and Marc A. Weiss. 2007. *Real Estate Development: Principles and Process.* 4th ed. Washington, DC: Urban Land Institute.

Moudon, Anne Vernez, Paul M. Hess, Mary Catherine Snyder, and Kiril Stanilov. 1997. *Effects of Site Design on Pedestrian Travel in Mixed-Use, Medium-Density Environments.* Final Report, Washington State Transportation Center; Washington State Department of Transportation. Federal Highway Administration.

Nelson, Arthur C. 2004. *Planner's Estimating Guide: Projection Land Use and Facility Needs.* Chicago: American Planning Association.

———. 2006. "Leadership in a New Era: Comment on 'Planning Leadership in a New Era'." *Journal of the American Planning Association* 72 (4): 393–409. http://dx.doi.org/10.1080/01944360608976762.

———. 2010. "Catching the Next Wave: Older Americans and the 'New Urbanism'." *Generations (San Francisco, Calif.)* 33 (4): 37–42.

———. 2013a. *A Home for Everyone.* Sacramento, CA: Council of Infill Builders.

———. 2013b. *Reshaping Metropolitan America: Development Trends and Opportunities to 2030.* Washington, DC: Island Press. http://dx.doi.org/10.5822/978-1-61091-222-8.

Nelson, Arthur C., Liza Bowles, Julian C. Juergensmeyer, and James C. Nicholas. 2008. *Impact Fees and Housing Affordability.* Washington, DC: Island Press.

Nelson, Arthur C., and James B. Duncan. 1995. *Growth Management Principles and Practice.* Chicago: American Planning Association.

Nelson, Arthur C., Reid Ewing, Matt Miller, Dejan Eskic, and Bruce Appleyard. 2013. "Bus Rapid Transit and Economic Development: Case Study of the Eugene-Springfield, Oregon, BRT System." *Journal of Public Transportation* 16 (3): 41–57.

Nelson, Arthur C., James C. Nicholas, and Julian C. Juergensmeyer. 2008. *Impact Fees: Principles and Practice of Proportionate-Share Development Fees.* Chicago: American Planning Association.

Northam, Robert M. 1971. "Vacant Urban Land in the American City." *Land Economics* 47 (4): 345–55. http://dx.doi.org/10.2307/3145071.

Oates, Wallace E., and Robert M. Schwab. 1996. *The Impact of Urban Land Taxation:*

*The Pittsburgh Experience.* Cambridge, MA: Lincoln Institute of Land Policy. Accessed December 12, 2013, at http://www.lincolninst.edu/subcenters/property-valuation-and-taxation-library/dl/oates_schwab.pdf.

Peiser, Richard B., and David Hamilton. 2012. *Professional Real Estate Development: The ULI Guide to the Business.* 3rd ed. Washington, DC: Urban Land Institute.

Petheram, Susan J., Arthur C. Nelson, Matt Miller, and Reid Ewing. 2013. "Use of the Real Estate Market to Establish Light Rail Station Catchment Areas." *Transportation Research Record: Journal of the Transportation Research Board* 2357 (1): 95–99.

Pitkin, John, and Dowell Myers. 2008. U.S. Housing Trends Generational Changes and the Outlook to 2050. Paper prepared for the Committee on the Relationships Among Development Patterns, Vehicle Miles Traveled, and Energy Consumption. Washington, DC: National Academy of Sciences, Transportation Research Board, and the Division on Engineering and Physical Sciences.

Pivo, Gary, and Jeffrey D. Fisher. 2010. "Income, Value and Returns to Socially Responsible Office Properties." *Journal of Real Estate Research* 32 (3): 243–70.

Port of Portland, Portland Development Commission, City of Portland, METRO. 2004. *Brownfield/Greenfield Development Cost Comparison Study.* Portland, OR: Port of Portland.

Robinson and Cole. 2007. *Urban Blight: An Analysis of State Blight Statutes and Their Implications for Eminent Domain Reform.* Washington, DC: National Association of Realtors.

Shoup, Donald. 1970. "The Optimal Timing of Urban Land Development." *Papers of the Regional Science Association* 25 (1): 33–44. http://dx.doi.org/10.1007/BF01935815.

Sobel, Lee, and Steven Bodzin. 2002. *Greyfields into Goldfields: Dead Malls Become Living Neighborhoods.* Chicago: Congress for the New Urbanism.

Story, Louis. 2012. "As Companies Seek Tax Deals, Governments Pay High Price." *New York Times,* December 1, 2012. Accessed May 2, 2014, at http://www.nytimes.com/2012/12/02/us/how-local-taxpayers-bankroll-corporations.html?pagewanted=all&_r=0.

Urban Land Institute. 2012. *Emerging Trends in Real Estate 2013.* Washington, DC: Urban Land Institute. Accessed January 1, 2013, at http://www.uli.org/wp-content/uploads/ULI-Documents/Emerging-Trends-in-Real-Estate-US-2013.pdf.

Williamson, June. 2013. *Designing Suburban Futures.* Washington, DC: Island Press. http://dx.doi.org/10.5822/978-1-61091-527-4.

Willson, Richard. 2013a. "Parking Reform Made Easy. *Access* 43:28–34. Accessed November 24, 2013, at http://www.uctc.net/access/43/access43_parking_reform.pdf.

———. 2013b. *Parking Reform Made Easy.* Washington, DC: Island Press.

# Index

# Island Press | Board of Directors

**Katie Dolan**
*(Chair)*
Conservationist

**Pamela B. Murphy**
*(Vice-Chair)*

**Merloyd Ludington Lawrence**
*(Secretary)*
Merloyd Lawrence, Inc.
and Perseus Books

**William H. Meadows**
*(Treasurer)*
Counselor and Past President
The Wilderness Society

---

**Decker Anstrom**
Board of Directors
Discovery Communications

**Stephen Badger**
Board Member
Mars, Inc.

**Terry Gamble Boyer**
Author

**Paula A. Daniels**
Founder
LA Food Policy Council

**Melissa Shackleton Dann**
Managing Director
Endurance Consulting

**Margot Paul Ernst**

**Anthony Everett**
Principle and Owner
HTE Marketing

**Russell Faucett**
General Partner
Barrington Partners

**Lisa A. Hook**
President and CEO
Neustar Inc.

**Mary James**
Prime Group, LLC

**Charles C. Savitt**
President
Island Press

**Alison Sant**
Cofounder and Partner
Studio for Urban Projects

**Ron Sims**
Former Deputy Secretary
US Department of Housing
and Urban Development

**Sarah Slusser**
Executive Vice President
GeoGlobal Energy LLC

**Deborah Wiley**
Chair
Wiley Foundation, Inc.